BUILDING YOUR DIGITAL UTOPIA

BUILDING YOUR DIGITAL UTOPIA

HOW TO CREATE DIGITAL BRAND EXPERIENCES THAT
SYSTEMATICALLY ACCELERATE GROWTH

FRANK COWELL

LIONCREST
PUBLISHING

BUILDING YOUR DIGITAL UTOPIA
*How to Create Digital Brand Experiences That
Systematically Accelerate Growth*

ISBN   978-1-5445-0614-2 *Hardcover*
           978-1-5445-0222-9 *Paperback*
           978-1-5445-0223-6 *Ebook*

For my wife and children: my "enablers" who have made huge sacrifices for me to be able to explore my craft and career. Everyone I'm able to impact owes them a debt of gratitude.

CONTENTS

INTRODUCTION

These days, people have more options than ever for promoting their brands and businesses. The landscape has become quite cluttered as countless point-and-click tools, service providers, and "gurus" have come on the scene claiming to make growing a company easy.

Paradoxically, all of these options are making things harder because of increased fragmentation. People are confronted with an endless array of channels and outreach methods that change almost every day. Unlike other skills, it's more difficult than ever to learn the crafts of marketing and sales, get good at them, and refine them over time, because tactics keep changing and there's a barrage of information that is impossible to keep up with.

It was my realization of this paradox that inspired me to find a better way.

NOISE AND FRAGMENTATION

When I began my career back in 1996, the Internet was just coming into its own, and the possibilities for promoting a business seemed mind-blowing. Back then, it was much easier to navigate available options because there weren't so many channels or endless platforms, apps, and software to consider.

While technology has been a great equalizer, giving more power and influence to small players, it has also accelerated everything. More people are empowered to participate, so there are more competitors than ever before. For a company looking to stand out, it can be extremely overwhelming.

How can you attract customers when there's so much noise? How do you differentiate yourself when so many competitors are vying for attention both on- and offline? Since it's easier than ever to get started, it's also easier for new entrants to come on the scene and blindside established competitors. Nobody is safe.

At the same time, customers have less loyalty to brands than they once did. The physical and mental cost of switching brands has never been smaller, so people are quick to make the jump, which has left companies scrambling to keep customers in an endless game of cat and mouse.

According to an article in *Forbes*, "The erosion of consumer loyalty among the most esteemed brands represents a changed philosophy of buying. The standard for brand switching is no longer the failure of a brand to perform, but rather its inability to seem like an entirely new and interesting option at every single purchase cycle."[1]

Seeing and experiencing this situation, I set out to create a framework that would help companies get back to basics, shifting away from the countless tactics and shiny objects that are so confusing. My goal was to find an effective way to raise awareness and engage potential customers amidst the noise. Above and beyond our product, how can we make people fall in love with our brand and create loyal, raving fans despite the increasing number of competitors?

A HOLISTIC GROWTH STRATEGY

In this book, I will present a holistic growth strategy that aligns your marketing, sales, and customer service teams into a single powerhouse growth team, systematically transforming strangers into raving fans in the digital age. The core focus is the belief that businesses must have a paradigm shift in how they think about sales, marketing,

---

1   Kathleen Kusek, "The Death of Brand Loyalty: Cultural Shifts Mean It's Gone Forever," *Forbes*, June 25, 2016, https://www.forbes.com/sites/kathleenkusek/2016/07/25/the-death-of-brand-loyalty-cultural-shifts-mean-its-gone-forever.

and service. Today, it's no longer about closing deals—it's about creating and elevating relationships with your target audience.

Not long ago, I met with the leaders of a company that has a whopping $2.5 million media budget, and in talking to them, I realized they had no idea what results they were getting for their money. In terms of real leads and opportunity, they had only acquired a handful of new prospects, but they kept spending the money with a "check the box" mentality.

"We're not sure what sort of return we're getting for our money," they said, "but we know we have to get our brand out there. It's part of the game we have to play to keep up with our competitors."

They're not alone. Many business leaders and marketers are doing things simply because they feel like they are supposed to. It is this mindset that I'm trying to change. The approach of many companies today is so wide and scattered that the effectiveness of their marketing activities is very low.

Talk to anyone doing digital marketing today, and they'll tell you that cost per click, cost per lead, and cost per acquisition are all going up, with no end in sight. Despite this, companies continue to go wide. Every time a new platform appears, they feel an obligation to embrace it.

"Oh, Snapchat is a thing now? I guess we'd better start using that platform, as well." That's the attitude.

The business community is so tactically obsessed that they've forgotten about the basics. They fail to put together a strategy centered on specific buyer personas that they have a real chance of making an impact on.

The problem has less to do with their content than with their approach. I find this is true in many areas of life, both personally and professionally. For example, I've met people who are miserable at work. They think their job—the *content*—is the problem when in reality it's their *approach* to the current job that needs to change. There are people struggling in unhappy personal relationships who think the solution is to end the relationship and find another one, but all they really need to change is their approach.

The same holds true when it comes to creating and growing an audience. So many people bounce from one platform to the next: "Blogging didn't work, let's try Instagram. Instagram didn't work, let's engage on LinkedIn." They go from tactic to tactic, activity to activity, constantly changing the content, but failing to change their overall approach.

This is a struggle at the executive level, with CEOs, COOs, and entrepreneurs constantly shifting tactics without seeing much return. It's a struggle among marketers as well: VPs, CMOs, and others who are tasked with growing brand awareness. It's also a source of tremendous stress and frustration on the sales side. At all levels, growing an audience has become harder, more confusing, and more expensive than ever.

My message for all of them is simple: If you will get clear on your approach to growth and relentlessly execute, you will begin to outpace your competitors. It won't matter if your approach is less than perfect—those who relentlessly execute a halfway decent plan will always outperform those who only execute when things are perfect. Relentless execution creates the most important factor for growth: *momentum*.

A FRAMEWORK FOR CHANGE

At one time, Fortune 100 companies got most of their valuation from factors like assets and contracted revenues—all things they could touch and validate. Today, a large percentage of valuation comes from good will, which is generated through brand. Even the biggest companies aren't immune to this change. If they're not careful, they can be blindsided by the marketplace access that average companies wield these days.

For example, Airbnb seemed to come out of nowhere, but it has made a serious dent in the hospitality industry, becoming a threat to even the most established and entrenched players. Suddenly, companies that have been around, in some instances, for a hundred years felt threatened by a start-up that didn't own a single set of bed linens but still managed to gain as much market share and valuation as the biggest players.

If you think you're going to beat your competitors on your offer alone, by simply out-featuring them, you're sadly mistaken. With such widespread access, it's too easy for a new upstart to swoop in and match your feature advantages. Any advantage will be extremely short-lived, so you can't bank on it.

There is one thing you can bank on, however: *brand*.

The future is a lot like the past—building brand will be our only path to long-term survival. As it turns out, brand makes everything easier: awareness, lead generation, customer conversion, and so much more. Building a brand creates raving fans and builds long-term value above and beyond the revenue on the books. In a world where buyers have no shortage of options, brand is what wins.

Those who know me know that I like to tell it like it is, so here's a dose of straight talk: If you can't embrace the idea that the future is about brand, then your days are numbered.

On the other hand, if you will begin to focus your efforts on creating meaning for a few select target audiences, a few select buyer personas, going deep with those people in a holistic way instead of aiming broadly, you will find yourself in a place of strength from which you can grow.

In the first part of this book, we will examine the problem. Something has broken in our approach to marketing our companies, and we need to acknowledge it. We've become like addicts, frantically chasing the next "fix," hoping that the next new tactic, platform, or idea will finally start to generate leads. We need a framework for change that will cure us of the addiction.

In the second part, we will examine the five core philosophies on which that framework stands, so you can get your marketing, sales, and customer service teams aligned with a *service-oriented mindset* and mission. You'll learn about the power of *hyper-specificity* and the importance of *slowing down to speed up*. You'll see how companies are developing clear buyer personas to focus their offerings and create *top-down optimization* for maximum performance, and you'll find the results you've been seeking through *commitment and consistency.*

Finally, in the third part of the book, having laid the philosophical foundation, we will examine the concrete steps for fully implementing this framework throughout your organization using the Digital Utopia Methodology. I will provide a practical plan for engaging both current and future customers at every relationship level to create a digital growth system.

Even if you choose not to fully engage with the framework presented in this book, if you simply heed the warning and embrace a strategic change in your organization— getting off the hamster wheel of endless tactics and focusing on creating brand—you will be poised to win.

PART ONE

MAKING THE CASE

CHAPTER ONE

PUT THE PAIN IN THE PAST

I understand your pain. I'm one of the founders of a marketing agency that has been in business for more than fifteen years, and in that time, we've had to make many adjustments in our approach, particularly in regard to digital marketing. We've seen the amazing amount of change brought about by the Internet and technology.

People have greater access than ever, and there's a low barrier of entry. Consequently, the number of new players is staggering. Practically anyone can start a marketing agency—all they need is a laptop and an Internet connection. They don't need an office because they can build their team virtually. All necessary software is extremely affordable, and all relevant information is freely available thanks to forums and online communities that freely share their knowledge.

As a result, the industry has become extremely noisy, which can be confusing for buyers. There are so many marketing agencies saying virtually the same thing that people don't know whom to trust. They can't tell who has real talent on their teams and who has simply created a slick website and has outsourced everything overseas. It's not enough for marketers to say, "We're very good at SEO. Trust us. Look at our great results." Everyone makes that claim.

Though I started my company fifteen years ago, I've been in sales and marketing for more than twenty-five years, and I've seen it all. I've watched as companies have adopted a short-term mindset, chasing every new tactic. They embrace the latest marketing trick, and when it doesn't pay off in thirty, sixty, or ninety days, they dump it and move on to something else. I've also experienced it firsthand—years of hopping from marketing tactic to marketing tactic with very little to show for it.

HubSpot, a leader in marketing, sales, and service enablement software, publishes an annual report on digital marketing, surveying marketing companies on a range of topics. They ask questions like: What are your plans for next year? What are you investing in? What are your concerns? What is your biggest challenge? To that last question, the most common answer year after year is, "Finding clients."

Think about that. Here are companies selling marketing services to help their customers find customers, and they can't even market themselves well enough to find their own. To me, that is the smoking gun that proves this industry is oversaturated.

If you want to become a dentist, you can't just rent some office space and hang a sign out front declaring yourself a dentist. The deception would soon be uncovered, either by a government agency or word of mouth from customers who learned the truth. But in the digital marketing industry, that's exactly what's happening. The barrier of entry is so low that just about anyone can hang a sign declaring themselves to be a skilled marketer.

It's happening everywhere.

THE PACE OF CHANGE

We live in a world where you could wake up one morning and discover that some major aspect of your industry has been automated with software, or you might find that some upstart company has developed a process that is far more efficient and affordable than yours. You can become obsolete at a moment's notice. That's the reality of technology today.

So often I find that companies fool themselves about how much better they are than their competition. They are convinced that they offer something truly special, yet to the marketplace, they don't look, act, or sound any different. There's so much noise from so many competitors that it's harder than ever to generate awareness, no matter how amazing a company might think it is. To differentiate, we all have to see past our own egos, step out of our own brands, and look at ourselves from the point of view of the marketplace.

At the same time, companies lack focus because there are so many options for engaging or reengaging target audiences. Awareness is difficult, differentiation is difficult, and focus is difficult.

Technology has been the great equalizer. Over time, it gets better, cheaper, and iterations come faster. The pace continues to accelerate. Until roughly the year 2000, the pace of technological change was happening on a scale that people could still wrap their heads around. Things were changing, technology was getting better, cheaper, and faster, but most people could deal with the changes.

Now, with the speed and availability of the Internet, acceleration is happening at a pace that humanity has never seen. A small team of people sitting in a one-bedroom apartment with nothing more than laptops and an Internet connection could build the next platform to rival Facebook.

If someone had wanted to unseat a major company fifty years ago, the amount of money, the number of people, and the logistics it would have required made it impossible for most people. Now, someone can come out of left field and, with very few resources, become a fierce competitor for an entire industry.

Our world has become incredibly small, and almost everyone has access. Ironically, with so much access, sameness abounds.

The first commercially available VCR was Ampex's VRX-1000, which came out in 1956 and was roughly the size of a washing machine. Though the VRX-1000 was an impressive technical achievement, it took years for VCR technology to gain widespread adoption or sell a million units. In fact, the technology didn't gain mass market traction until 1975, but the real boom didn't happen until the 1980s.[2] These days, however, a new technology can reach a million users within a matter of days.

---

2   Johnnie L. Roberts, "The VCR Boom: Prices Drop as Their Popularity Continues to Grow," *Chicago Tribune*, September 22, 1985, https://www.chicagotribune.com/news/ct-xpm-1985-09-22-8503040687-story.html.

Thirty years ago, if you wanted world-class software to power your business, it would cost a huge amount of money, no matter your industry. In 2000, I had a job with a web development company that had created a content management system. The cost for installation of the software, once you factored in plug-ins and modules, ran as high as $50,000. On top of that, clients had to pay a hefty annual license.

While there are still expensive, enterprise-quality content management systems, most of those clients could do everything they were doing in 2000 using just Word-Press today, which is absolutely free. Think about that. In just a handful of years, we went from companies paying $50,000 for content management software to using WordPress for free to do the same thing.

In 2000, if you wanted to run powerful web analytics, you had to pay a company like Urchin, who would use their own software to analyze your traffic. They were a real company making real revenue to analyze website traffic. Then Google came along and turned web analytics into a free service, and suddenly paid services like Urchin were obsolete.

While you can still pay for advanced or highly specialized analytics, most of what Urchin provided is now available for free. What used to be a resource limited to companies with significant financial resources in 2000 is now available to absolutely everyone. Not only is Google free, but it is extremely powerful, and it's constantly being improved.

In 2000, high quality accounting software could cost thousands of dollars. Today, businesses have access to QuickBooks Online for prices ranging from $20 to $60 a month.[3] That's very cheap for powerful professional accounting software.

For internal communications, twenty years ago, large companies would often pay to develop their own proprietary systems. Today, there's Slack, which offers a free version that is suitable for many companies. You can host your own corporate domain for emails with Google Apps for Work, and Google also offers a full office productivity suite called G Suite that takes the place of Microsoft Word, Excel, and PowerPoint. Then there's Google Cloud, which offers online storage for an amazing price that starts at $5 per user per month.

All of these affordable online tools and resources would have been unthinkable twenty years ago. The average user has access to so much power at such reasonable prices that it has completely changed the landscape in every industry.

---

3   Crystalynn Shelton, "QuickBooks Online vs Desktop: Which Is Right for You in 2019?" *Fit Small Business*, January 31, 2019, https://fitsmallbusiness.com/quickbooks-online-vs-desktop/.

IDEAS SPREAD FAST

Because of the empowerment brought on by technological changes, ideas spread faster than ever. Through LinkedIn, Facebook, Instagram, and other platforms, as well as industry-specific forums, anyone can disseminate ideas around the world. There's no more "secret sauce." In fact, there are very few industries in which companies can contain information. Some have given up trying, as when Elon Musk removed the patents for much of Tesla's technology and made the information open source.

Despite this, when I meet with company leaders, they tend to get nervous as soon as we start delving into their business processes. They don't want to speak openly about their "secret sauce" because they're afraid of competitors finding out. I have to remind them, "Your competitors probably already know your secrets. After all, you already know all about your competitors, and you mock their big secrets."

Legendary marketer Al Reis, co-author of the book *Positioning*, has pointed out that differentiating yourself based on product advantages doesn't get you far anymore. Marketing people tend to aggressively advertise their differences.

As Reis puts it, "But what happens when the competition catches up? At that point, many companies go back to the drawing board and see if they can find another difference they can promote. And guess what: All they do is confuse consumers who can't differentiate yesterday's slogan from today's slogan. Exclusivity is not a long-term advantage. If competitors don't copy your point of difference, consumers assume it's not that important."[4]

Even the godfather of brand positioning says you can no longer rely on trying to outdo your competitors on product features.

Growth has become a liability, because the bigger you get, the more likely it is you've built an infrastructure based on today's model, today's technology, and today's client mood. When all of those things change *tomorrow*, it's not going to be easy to adapt. This is why big companies have more trouble evolving with the pace of change.

It's the reason why Hilton didn't invent Airbnb. Instead, it was invented by a couple of roommates in San Francisco who were looking for a way to make a few extra bucks after their landlord raised the rent.[5] It's the reason why the Taxicab Association didn't invent Uber. Instead, it was invented by an entrepreneur who was appalled at

---

4   Al Ries, "Differentiation Will Get You Only So Far," *AdAge*, February 11, 2014, https://adage.com/article/al-ries/differentiation/239693/.

5   Biz Carson, "How 3 guys turned renting an air mattress in their apartment into a $25 billion company," *Business Insider*, February 23, 2016, https://www.businessinsider.com/how-airbnb-was-founded-a-visual-history-2016-2.

paying a private driver $800 and wanted to find a cheaper way to get around.[6]

Big companies tend to build an elaborate infrastructure to support the way they do business, which makes it almost impossible to change. They're in the business of doing business, when they should be in the business of serving their customers.

YOUR MENTAL MODEL

There's a mental model exercise I like to walk companies through. It's very simple. I ask them to complete the following sentence with two or three words:

We are in the business of...

Your answer should be built around your audience. What outcome are you trying to deliver to your target customer? That desired outcome is your mental model, and if you're not obsessed with it, you run the risk of becoming too static. If your focus drifts to *what* you're doing instead of *who* you're serving, you will be slower to adapt. This risk increases the bigger your company becomes.

---

6   Alyson Shontell, "All Hail the Uber Man! How Sharp-Elbowed Salesman Travis Kalanick Became Silicon Valley's Newest Star," *Business Insider*, January 11, 2014, https://www. businessinsider.com/uber-travis-kalanick-bio-2014-1.

The net result is *sameness*. In almost any industry, buyers can get roughly the same thing for roughly the same price, whether they're buying a hamburger or enterprise marketing software.

Without the right mindset, established companies are at a disadvantage. Unless they change their approach, they run the risk of being blindsided by a new start-up that invents the next thing the marketplace falls in love with. Consider the famous example of Kodak, which was an iconic brand in America for generations. How did such a famous brand find itself in deep financial trouble to the point of bankruptcy?

In my opinion, it's because they weren't committed to the right mental model. Their focus was on doing business using established procedures, processes, and people. Had they focused instead on delivering what their target customers wanted, they might have navigated the profound changes in the market.

Had their mental model been, "We're in the business of life's memories," they never would have held on so long, or so tightly, to photographic film as it became obsolete. Instead, they would have been looking for better ways to meet their customers' need. They had enough intelligent, creative people working for them that they could have remained on the cutting edge, ushering in the digital revolution. Maybe they would have invented the next big social media platform as another way to fulfill their mental model.

How does a big, established company like Kodak get blindsided? By being obsessed with the *things* of their business rather than the *concept* of their business. When they focus on the concept, then they are more likely to explore new ways to achieve it. Can you see the difference in approach between saying, "We're in the business of film," versus, "We're in the business of life's memories"?

Remember, you are never in the business of the *medium*, you are in the business of the *concept*. Most business leaders fail to understand this.

It is imperative that you begin thinking this way, making decisions and taking actions accordingly, because if you don't, someone else will.

TACTICAL ADDICTS

If you don't understand the concept of your business, if you don't have a clear mental model, then every new "tactic of the day" is going to seem attractive to you. Since you don't really understand what your business is all about, it will be easy to chase the latest marketing trick. When that tactic doesn't work out right away, you will be tempted to dump it and move on to the next thing. Soon, you start to look like an addict, constantly chasing another short-term fix.

There are three things you have to acknowledge:

First, you are one of many in your industry. Don't underestimate your competition.

Second, no matter how great you think your product is, it's not enough to separate you from the noise, because your competitors can and will quickly match any advantages you currently possess. Buyers have plenty of options, so your product alone won't cut it, no matter how great it is.

Third, chasing the latest sales or marketing trick isn't a solution. Clever campaigns, cute ads, great brand identity, expensive commercials, Super Bowl ads, crafty sales tactics, and clever contracting terms don't cut it anymore. The effectiveness of these kinds of tactics is at an all-time low, and there's no possibility of returning to the glory days.

What's the solution?

As I said earlier, it's about building brand. Brand is our only way forward. However, I don't mean *brand* in the traditional sense of the word. What do I mean? Let's find out.

CHAPTER TWO

COMMIT TO BUILDING YOUR BRAND

When I talk about *building brand*, a lot of things are probably conjured in your mind that have nothing to do with the solution provided in this book. You might think about logos, taglines, vehicle wraps, billboards, and other kinds of advertising. However, I'm talking about something much bigger.

When I talk about brand, I'm referring to the *reputation* that walks into the room before you do. Everything your company says and does, or chooses not to do, contributes to that reputation.

As I've said, buyers have so many options these days that

it is hard for any company to differentiate. The market is saturated, so how can you stand out? How can you differentiate your brand to your target audience?

I'm not suggesting you don't need advertising. Far from it. You do need traditional forms of advertising, but those aren't the things that are most effective at building brand today, and if you don't build your brand, you will always be in a hamster wheel of marketing activities. You will be constantly chasing every opportunity without building any real equity.

A company that wants to generate leads could hire a call center or a telemarketing lead-generation firm to call constantly day after day, and they *might* generate the leads they desire. However, that methodology is becoming less effective. If you pour all of your energy into it, it will eventually run its course, and, more importantly, it provides zero equity. In other words, when the calling stops, everything stops.

BUILDING BRAND TODAY

So, what's the key to effectively building brand today? Ultimately, it's all about relationships. It's about building real human connections by moving toward human-to-human interactions as much as possible. Everything stems from that human connection, and the more you invest in making those connections, the more momentum you will build in creating a brand that is differentiated from the oversaturated market.

It's not the things on your invoice that build your brand. In his book *Start with Why*, Simon Sinek talks about the importance of the *why* over the *what*, but I believe companies should start with *who* and then consider the *how*. I believe the *how* is where you create tangible differentiation—specifically a *how* that is built around a specific *who*.

You can inspire people with your *why*, but if you don't develop an effective *how*, your *why* won't matter. When you invoice a customer, your *how* doesn't appear on the invoice, and it doesn't appear on a receipt. It will never appear on the income side of a profit and loss statement—it will only ever appear as expenses—but it is the thing that matters most.

To invest in *how*, you need a long-term view. To put it another way, it needs to become a "lifestyle" that permeates your entire organization. It's this overarching concept that people will be willing to pay for, and it is wrapped up in your *who*. It commercializes what you do as a company and makes it valuable.

Consider the success of McDonald's. One can compare a McDonald's cheeseburger to a steak at a nice restaurant and judge it harshly, but that's not the company's concept. Their concept is to provide fast, tasty, affordable food on a consistent basis. When you go there, you know exactly what you're going to get, and, to a large degree, you are paying for that concept.

Some people look down on McDonald's because it's unhealthy, and everyone knows that if you eat there every day, it's not good for you. However, providing a healthy experience isn't their concept either. They're not competing with health food restaurants. Everyone understands the concept of McDonald's—after all, they were pioneers of the *fast food* movement—so customers know the experience they are going to get there. Nobody says, "Should we go to the high-end restaurant on the hill that sells a $55 burger topped with truffle oil and champagne steam-melted Gruyere or should we go to the McDonald's on the corner for a Big Mac and fries?" The two restaurants aren't competitors because their concepts are completely different—both their *who* and their *how*.

This is why the mental model of your brand is so important. When your concept is clear, then your commercial value will be clear to customers who value that concept. Immediately, you will stand apart from other companies that might, on the surface, seem to offer a similar product with similar features.

Your concept is the seed of your brand, but until it permeates your entire organization, it won't guide everything you do. Your team has to get excited about it. They have to walk through the doors every morning ready to innovate and fulfill the concept.

Southwest Airlines is another company with a clear concept. In fact, in a famous story, they received a series of complaint letters from a customer who was disappointed about the things the company *didn't* offer. As told by Alexander Kjerulf, founder and "Chief Happiness Officer" of Woohoo Inc.:

> One woman who frequently flew on Southwest was constantly disappointed with every aspect of the company's operation. In fact, she became known as the "Pen Pal" because after every flight she wrote in with a complaint.
>
> She didn't like the fact that the company didn't assign seats; she didn't like the absence of a first-class section; she didn't like not having a meal in flight; she didn't like Southwest's boarding procedure; she didn't like the flight attendants' sporty uniforms and the casual atmosphere.[7]

When the customer relations team couldn't assuage her

---

[7]   Alex, "TOP 5 REASONS WHY 'THE CUSTOMER IS ALWAYS RIGHT' IS WRONG," *The Chief Happiness Officer Blog*, July 12, 2006, https://positivesharing.com/2006/07/why-the-customer-is-always-right-results-in-bad-customer-service/.

disgruntlement, her case was bumped up to the CEO of Southwest, Herb Kelleher. He dashed off a quick response to the customer that got right to the point:

Dear Mrs. Crabapple,

We will miss you.

Love, Herb.[8]

The CEO knew the company's concept, and he was crystal clear about the value of that concept for their target buyer. He wasn't trying to be all things to all people or compete with airlines that operated under a different mental model.

Marketing legend Dan Kennedy, who has been called "The Professor of Harsh Reality," likes to say that great brands repel as much as they attract. Sadly, companies today are working furiously to appease everybody. They are terrified that a customer will say something negative about them on social media, and this fear makes them generic and mediocre.

I'm not suggesting that companies should try to offend people, but when a brand has a clear concept, they are going to repel certain audiences and attract others. That's

---

8   Ibid.

not something to be afraid of. On the contrary, it is *necessary* for differentiation.

THE RELATIONSHIP MINDSET

In order to build a brand, you have to build meaningful relationships, but how do you do that in today's digital world? How do you create and elevate relationships if you're not constantly in front of your customers?

To do that, you have to start thinking of yourself as a media company. When you think of yourself as a media company, you take a radically different approach to everything you do. What is the core of a media company? Content.

Of course, many marketing experts have emphasized the importance of content in marketing and brand-building, so what I'm suggesting isn't new. However, when you combine your content with the approach that I discuss in this book, you're going to find yourself creating exactly the kind of engagement you've been hoping for. Your competitors will be jealous of the level of engagement you produce.

In fact, one of the problems with content today is that most of it is boring and ineffective because companies aren't clear on their mental model and their target buyer.

When you combine the three—a clear concept, a target buyer, and creative content—you get a potent mix.

As I said earlier, this is another example of a *how* built around a *who*.

SOME COMPANIES ARE DOING IT RIGHT

Are there companies that have done this well? Certainly. Consider the example of Starbucks. Their commercial concept is called "The Third Place," and the idea is for the company to become a third place in the daily lives of their customers: Home, Work, Starbucks.

In a *Fast Company* article, a Starbucks manager explained it this way: "We want to provide all the comforts of your home and office. You can sit in a nice chair, talk on your phone, look out the window, surf the web...oh, and drink coffee, too."[9] Notice that selling coffee isn't even first on the list.

You go to work, then you head home. That's the standard routine of a working person. But maybe between home and work you meet up with a friend or colleague at Starbucks. Maybe it becomes your regular pitstop on the way

---

9   Matthew Dollinger, "Starbucks, 'The Third Place,' and Creating the Ultimate Customer Experience," *Fast Company*, June 11, 2008, https://www.fastcompany.com/887990/starbucks-third-place-and-creating-ultimate-customer-experience.

to work in the morning, or maybe it's the place you take a break in the middle of the day. In that sense, it's a lot like the pub in UK culture or the coffeehouse tradition in Italy.

Starbucks is so clear about this concept that they post it prominently on their website, where they describe the concept as, "A place for conversation and a sense of community. A third place between work and home...It's not unusual to see people coming to Starbucks to chat, meet up, or even work. We're a neighborhood gathering place, a part of the daily routine—and we couldn't be happier about it. Get to know us and you'll see: we are so much more than what we brew."[10]

Everything they do, including the content they create, is wrapped around that concept.

Fortunately, you don't need to have the massive budget of Starbucks to achieve this. Even if you can't produce massive volume, you can begin to think strategically as long as you have a clear concept of who you are. When you can create value for your target buyer, you will cease to be unheard in the sea of noise that is today's marketplace.

---

10   "Company Information," *Starbucks*, https://www.starbucks.com/about-us/
      company-information.

YOUR DIGITAL ECOSYSTEM

At this point, you might be thinking, "I understand what you're saying, but there are so many options and tools and resources—it's overwhelming!" Yes, even if you have the right mindset—a clear concept and a target buyer—the implementation can be overwhelming. The only way to get a handle on it is to have a framework to build on.

That's what I want to give you in this book. I want to provide you with a working framework, supported by five core philosophies, that can guide you in implementing your strategy. What you build on that framework will become the digital ecosystem in which you implement specific campaigns to reach your target audience.

I use the term *ecosystem* because you can't approach this as if it were a machine. With a machine, you build it once, give it some oil and fuel from time to time, and just let it run. That's not the approach I'm advocating. In nature, an ecosystem, unlike a machine, is a dynamic community of interacting organisms, and the health of an ecosystem is measured by *energy flow*.

When you have a balanced ecosystem, you have greater flow, and the entire ecosystem thrives. However, that balance is dynamic because individual elements within the ecosystem are constantly changing. Humidity rises and falls, weather patterns change, migratory patterns adjust and evolve. Almost nothing is static.

Even without the intervention of humans, an ecosystem can become out of balance. Fluctuations in weather patterns or natural features can produce massive changes. This concept is called *the butterfly effect*, which is defined as a phenomenon in which minute localized changes can produce big effects in a complex system.

All of the tools, resources, and platforms we have at our disposal today work together very much like an ecosystem. Balance is a delicate thing, with elements constantly shifting, and we have to take into account variability. The elements at play interact with one another and create ripple effects. When a specific audience interacts with your ecosystem, it creates widespread, possibly unpredictable results, and that audience, in turn, is influenced by elements outside of your ecosystem—and probably outside of your control.

There is a tremendous amount of complexity. That's why you can't just hire a marketing firm and a sales superstar and then walk away to focus on other things. Your ecosystem is constantly changing, which makes your implementation far more challenging than you might expect.

How can you even begin to get your arms around it?

To do so, I believe you need two things: a set of overarching philosophies and a strategic blueprint. I want to provide you with both. Now, it's entirely possible that you already have a growth blueprint that you follow. If so, take the core philosophies that I share and apply them to the blueprint. I believe you will see massive improvement. In this book, I'll be introducing you to the Digital Utopia Blueprint.

The approach I share here is *not* the "be-all end-all." However, it is an approach that I've developed and matured, and I know from much experience that it works. If you're currently disappointed with the results you're getting, I believe the approach I teach in this book will produce noticeably better results.

PART TWO

FIVE CORE PHILOSOPHIES: THE FOUNDATION

CHAPTER THREE

SERVICE MINDSET

A service-driven mindset has to permeate your entire organization. Every single member of your team must understand their role in bringing your concept—your mental model—to life. It's not just the job of one department.

During my stint in the U.S. Marine Corps, I vividly remember a time during combat training when they sat us down and said, "Look around at one another. Some of you are black, some of you are white, some of you are brown, and so on. But from this point forward, you're no longer any of those colors. From now on, you're all just shades of green." It was their first step in making sure we knew we were a brotherhood.

Building on that concept, they added, "It doesn't matter what your job is, you are absolutely critical to the mission."

In other words, if you're lugging around the .50 caliber, which is a heavy and unwieldy piece of equipment, your purpose is to get it to its destination in one piece and in proper working order, so the next person can operate the equipment properly. That makes you critical to the mission. If your job is bulk fuel, you're more than just the military's version of a gas station attendant. You are helping to keep vehicles fueled so they can get where they need to go. That makes you critical to the mission.

In the same way, everyone in your organization, no matter their specific task, should understand their importance to the mission. To do that, however, the mission must be crystal clear, and the executives must embody it.

A SELFLESS SPIRIT

Having a selfless spirit means putting others before you. Every member of your team should be committed to serving your target audience, not merely responding to them. Serving is proactive, while responding is reactive.

This mindset of service isn't focused solely on customers. Instead, your focus should be your target audience. That means you are actively looking for ways to engage and serve those who are seeking out what you have to offer, those who are actively engaging with your marketing or sales team, those who are currently customers, and even those who have been your customers for many years.

When you embrace this selfless spirit, then your marketing and sales departments become an intrinsic part of your customer service, but they are treating *potential* customers as if they are already customers. Think of it this way:

You're providing customer service to people who don't yet realize they're your customers.

That's the level of service you should be providing to your entire target audience.

What does this look like for each segment of your organization? It looks like everyone working together in a common mission. What if marketing's job wasn't to create marketing-qualified leads (MQLs) for the sales team, but to simply serve the target audience, almost as if they were in a nonprofit organization? If that were the case, how would they define the mission of their department differently? What kind of content would they produce? Chances are, they would adopt a radically different approach.

I'm not suggesting companies *shouldn't* look at return on investment (ROI), or that marketing teams *aren't*

SERVICE MINDSET · 51

accountable for generating MQLs. I'm simply suggesting that a change in mindset will produce more effective and meaningful marketing. With a mindset of service, your team will produce content of greater relevance for your target audience.

HubSpot is a great example of this. To participate in their training, you don't actually have to be a HubSpot customer. You can learn about various marketing, sales, and service methodologies, get certified, and become an even greater value to your employer without purchasing HubSpot's software. This was a flash of brilliance on the part of the company's leadership team, and it shows how a mindset of service permeates the organization.

Your sales team should also embrace this mindset and start looking at their pipelines accordingly. If the percentage of prospects who move from one stage to the next aren't what you're hoping for, instead of trying to figure out which salespeople to blame, try to understand why prospects don't naturally move forward on their own.

Are you failing to service them in a way that's so valuable that the next step is natural and logical? In fact, it should be so natural and logical that moving forward to the next step becomes *their* idea.

Don't blame individual salespeople. Instead, look at the whole team's approach as part of your overall system. Have you failed to build service into every aspect of your organization? A prospect should already be treated like a customer long before they ever move from the first stage to the second. If you service them well, thinking specifically about what they need rather than your sales pipeline, they will naturally move to the next part of the sales funnel.

I'm not suggesting you shouldn't measure your conversion rate or close rate. I'm not suggesting you shouldn't look at the cost of customer acquisition. In fact, as you'll see later in the book, conversion rates and cost of customer acquisition are important to define. What I'm suggesting is that your disappointing results are, first and foremost, the consequence of a missing mindset. That's the first place to look. Shift from *selling* to *servicing*, from *closing deals* to *elevating relationships*, and you will start making progress.

MEETING INCREASED DEMAND

One of my associates, Dan Tyre, Sales Director for HubSpot and co-author of the book *Inbound Organization*, shared his own perspective with me on a service-oriented mindset. Here is what he had to say:

Everything changed when customer buying habits moved online. As customers became more educated, they began relying less on salespeople for information, but at the same time, they began expecting a more personalized approach and a higher level of service. The companies that leaned into an inbound philosophy gained a huge competitive advantage, as they were discovered more often by new buyers looking for help. The companies that greeted prospects with helpful information earned trust and made it easier for prospects to buy.

Do you remember the good old days? I'm referring, of course, to 2006. In the good old days of 2006, people had reasonable expectations, less noise, and more time to consider a purchasing decision.

Today, the competition, the number of channels that companies have to navigate in order to connect with people, and the world of instant gratification are forcing companies to improve their game. If you're still running your business without understanding how to meet the increased demand of the market, it's only going to get more difficult.

Frank's approach is designed to help companies scale. He achieves this in a few key ways:

*1) **A customer service mindset**. Know your customer, know **what** they want, **how** they want it, and deliver the right information at the right level at the right time without regard to*

*remuneration. Treat people like human beings—helping them
without spam or a pushy attitude.*

2) *"**The riches are in the niches.**" If you try to help everyone,
you won't be able to help anyone. Would you hire a foot doctor
to replace your spleen? No, you want a gastroenterologist to
treat your spleen.*

3) ***Move at the customer's pace.** This is hard to do. As my
friend and colleague, Dan Vivian, HubSpot's Channel Account
Manager, put it, 'It's better for customers to move on **their**
timeline. You can do a bit of incentivizing after they make the
decision, but trying to subvert their clear timeline is a high risk.
Instead, understand the influences and requirements, build a
diagram of all the activities, and make sure everyone understands value first.'*

4) ***Top-down commitment.** My co-author Todd Hockenberry
is famous for saying, 'To do inbound, you must be outbound,'
which is all about creating a culture of helping, a culture code,
an inbound operating system, and empowering employees to
do their best work.*

5) ***Inbound is a process.** Rather than approaching inbound
as a marketing tactic, view it as a mindset and strategy.*

HubSpot is a perfect example of this. They know exactly
whom they're trying to help, and they hyper-target pros-

pects to make sure everyone who becomes a customer has a good experience. The company leans heavily into the customer service mindset starting from the moment a prospect emerges, whether by phone, chat, email, website, or paid advertising.

The company leads with free help and education, and they have a tailored approach to providing content that relates to individual prospects. Salespeople have to understand what clients like and don't like, which is why HubSpot salespeople take a progressive approach and act more like consultants.

HubSpot provides free software so customers can try before they buy, along with free training, tutorials, consultations, group training, and problem-solving. It's a philosophy that has produced fast growth over the last ten years.

CLEANING UP YOUR SALES PIPELINE

If you approach the sales process with a service mindset, then your first step with any prospect is to determine whether or not they are a good fit for your company's offerings. The prospect should be able to convince *you* that they're a good fit.

If you don't approach sales with that lens, you end up

putting far too many people into your sales pipeline by making them look like they are a good fit. In sales, we call this "happy ears." In other words, we hear what we want to hear.

Instead, you need to accept that you have a very defined target audience that finds value in what you have to offer. Most of the people you meet will not be a good fit and don't belong in your sales pipeline. When you first engage people, your job is to help them find the right next step, rather than trying to push them along the funnel.

Most salespeople act as if taking the next step with their brand is the only option, but in reality, there are many options on the table. This is why so many sales pipelines are inflated or, at least, filled with opportunities that aren't real.

Your job is to get a prospect pointed in the right direction. That direction might be toward your company, or it might not be. You should only point people in your direction if it's right for that individual. Otherwise, help them find a better way to go.

If you adopt that mindset, not only will you build your brand by putting goodwill into the marketplace, but your sales pipelines will be far more accurate. Then you will be able to spend more time on the people who are a good fit for your offerings.

If someone is a good fit, helping them take the next step in your pipeline isn't merely a sales effort—it's a *service* effort. You know taking that next step will help them achieve their own goals. Many salespeople wind up frustrated because they spend so much time with bad leads—so-called "tire kickers"—in their pipeline. They never should have moved those leads into their pipeline in the first place.

CUSTOMER REACTION DEPARTMENT

Since companies don't view customer service as part of brand building, they fail to see the role it can play in generating new opportunities and revenue. Instead, they approach it as merely a necessary expense. Success is measured by metrics like call length, which encourages team members to move through customer calls as fast as possible. To save money, many companies now outsource their call centers to places that make communication even more difficult.

This is the same kind of thinking that causes companies to understaff the service department, creating long hold times, or install complex Interactive Voice Response (IVR) systems that require callers to press multiple buttons as they navigate through automated menus. In practice, customer service departments are little more than customer *reaction* departments, and most customers find their interactions unpleasant.

Fortunately, some companies are doing it right.

Take DigitalMarketer, for example. They have created a private Facebook community for existing customers to discuss problems and share tips and solutions with each other. Employees participate in these discussions with customers. They also produce free webinars on a variety of relevant topics. Even the CEO, Ryan Deiss, regularly participates in online conversations, giving advice, responding to questions, and connecting with customers. It's not uncommon to see him posting in discussion threads late into the night.

As a result, DigitalMarketer has created raving fans who champion the company and even correct their detractors. I know because I am one of their fans, and my company is one of their certified partners.

IKEA offers planning tools to help customers design their office and home spaces. As they explain on their website, "Plan your dream kitchen, your perfect office or your wardrobe storage system before making a commitment. Play with colors, styles, sizes and configurations to plan your way to perfection with our easy to use tools...Try as many designs as you want and get a detailed product list with price."[11]

---

11   "About Our Products: Planning Tools," *IKEA*, https://www.ikea.com/ms/en_US/customer-service/about-our-products/planning-tools/index.html.

These planning tools could be a source of revenue for the company, but they've decided to offer them as a free resource to their customers and potential customers. IKEA also provides free tips and advice in-store. They even have a consultation service that will help a customer complete their home or office design.

A UNIFIED MISSION

Your marketing, sales, and customer service teams are each going to have their own processes, but all three teams should meet regularly to unify around one mission. When this fails to happen, these teams can develop adversarial relationships—a situation that is not uncommon in the corporate world.

During these meetings, your teams can discuss ways to service your target audience, regardless of what stage they're in. Your customer service department will have valuable insight and stories to share with both marketing and sales, stories that can be transformed into public-facing material or training materials for the sales team.

Likewise, your sales team will have stories to share with marketing and customer service that can provide insight about what's happening in the marketplace. After all, your salespeople are the ones hearing directly from customers about the frustrations they experience buying from companies like yours.

Marketing can also provide valuable input about the information customers are looking for, such as popular search terms, buying patterns, and market shifts. Working together, these three teams will become stronger, more relevant, and develop a differentiated approach to your target audience. Your executive team should be involved in this as well, making sure everyone is working together toward shared goals.

All of these stories become sources of extremely valuable content, a critical component to your *digital ecosystem*. We'll explore this in greater detail later in the book.

CHAPTER FOUR

HYPER-SPECIFICITY

What makes business leaders avoid specificity? To use a trendy acronym, it's *FOMO*: fear of missing out. They're afraid that if they get too specific with their message and targeting, they will miss out on some of the audiences they serve.

"Shouldn't we also be engaging with this audience over here?" they think.

At the same time, their company might have ten different things they could offer the marketplace, and they want to make sure they communicate all of them. However, the truth is they only excel at a couple of those offers.

When you create a message that isn't hyper-specific, it

becomes harder for people to decipher who the message is intended for. The message becomes muddy and generic, rather than speaking clearly to a specific audience. That's what Dan Kennedy means when he says a great brand repels as much as it attracts, but it's a fact that many businesspeople have failed to grasp.

If you want to stand out, you must be willing to polarize. If you want to attract, you must be willing to repel.

If you can't get specific about who you serve—if you continue trying to serve a dozen different audiences—you're going to have trouble competing in the marketplace, and you're going to find it increasingly difficult to grow.

FOCUS ON YOUR BUYER PERSONA

When we talk about hyper-specificity, we're talking about how you engage through your go-to-market activities. You may have more than one buyer persona, and that's fine. However, your go-to-market campaigns need to become much more specific.

I recommend hyper-focusing on one buyer persona and making sure that person is crystal clear. Understand them on a deep emotional level. Who is this person? Where do they live? What is their lifestyle like? How do they think? What is their job title? What is their level of education?

What questions do they have? What are their biggest challenges and frustrations? How are you going to change their lives?

When you clarify a buyer persona, you can engage the marketplace without trying to attract a broad range of people with varying interests and needs. Instead, you can focus each campaign on one type of person, honing in on one pain point.

Ask yourself, "What is the one pain point my organization is really good at addressing?" Even before customers do business with you, you can provide information and resources to begin helping with that pain point. In doing so, you convey the idea that you're so good at solving that pain point that your help goes beyond your service offering.

If you're a B2B company, you may be trying to engage with a buying cohort, but your messaging should still lead with one person in mind. If you have multiple people in the cohort that you need to connect with, then you will need multiple campaigns, each one going after a specific individual. This will always be far more effective than a general message that is meant to take in multiple people. To find the one person you need most, determine which individual in the cohort cares the most about solving the specific pain point.

Some companies have done a masterful job at identifying a clear buyer persona for their messaging. Consider the manufacturing company HOLDRITE, which produces industrial plumbing equipment. Their marketing director, Darlene Byrne, has developed a buyer persona named Frank the Foreman. Everyone in the company has come to know Frank the Foreman extremely well, and they are very specific about serving him.

They are so obsessed with helping Frank that when it comes time to develop new solutions, they find people who best represent that buyer persona and bring them into the conversation, letting them participate in research and development.

When you have this kind of clarity—when you make it about the person and not the product—then even a "boring" product like industrial plumbing becomes exciting. You have fun stories to tell because you know the person you're talking about, and you're very good at innovating solutions for them.

FOCUS ON YOUR OFFERING

Once you have a clear idea of whom you're engaging with, and what pain point you're addressing, you can develop a clear understanding of what you have to offer to solve that pain point for that person. Remember, this isn't about all of your offerings. You need to narrow your focus to one or two specific offerings that create conceptual value for your buyer persona.

Bear in mind, what you lead with may not be your biggest economic opportunity. Rather, it should be the offering that resonates most clearly, or best solves, that specific pain point for that specific buyer persona. You're leading with clarity that will resonate with that person.

How can you decide which offering to focus on? Making that decision will require some honest discussion within your entire executive team. Which of your customers are happiest? Which are getting the best results and have the highest retention? Which customers refer your company the most, increase their spending the most, and deepen their relationship with you?

The answers are sitting there in your existing client base. It's all right in front of you. You don't need to do expensive market research to figure it out.

You can certainly survey your customer base to obtain this information. In fact, it's always a good idea to survey your customers. However, you'd be surprised how much you can learn by inviting small groups of customers to a series of coffee meetings and talking with them. This kind of face-to-face research is easy to arrange and very affordable. Plus, it contributes to long-term relationship building.

What it boils down to is this: The more specific you get in your targeting, messaging, and offering, the better your results will be. Yes, the size of your audience will shrink as a direct result of specificity, but your outcome will be greater.

CHAPTER FIVE

SLOW DOWN TO SPEED UP

Companies often try to move too quickly with potential customers. For example, a company might have a white paper or an e-book for free download on their website, and the immediate follow-up from either the company or a salesperson is, "Contact us to find out about our services."

This is the wrong approach. Just because someone downloaded an e-book from your website doesn't mean they're interested in buying anything from you. They might become interested down the road, but you can't assume they're already buyers just from a single point of contact.

You have to acknowledge that fact and respect it. I'm not suggesting that follow-ups shouldn't happen. After all,

I'm a salesperson at heart. However, you have to respect the context. Put yourself in the customer's shoes. If you'd just downloaded a free e-book, would that mean you're ready to become a buyer? Probably not.

If you're obsessed with people instead of your offering, you'll approach these situations with a different mindset. Think of it like dating. It takes time to go from a first date to a committed relationship, and most of the time, you take it slow to ensure a real connection forms. Plus, you don't want to scare your date off by being too needy or pushy from the beginning.

Imagine being on a first date with the conversation flowing and you suddenly say, "I envision us married, living in a beautiful three-story home in the suburbs. We've got a picket fence, a dog named Fido, and a couple of kids: Billy and Madison. We take them to soccer on the weekends and cheer them on. Doesn't that sound nice? Let's make it happen!" If you start talking like that on the first date, the relationship is probably going nowhere fast. If anything, your date will think you're incredibly weird or creepy.

But that's exactly what companies do all the time. "Oh, you downloaded our e-book? How about you become a committed customer for life?" That's not much different than saying, "Oh, you talked to me for the first time? How about we get married right now?" We have to stop doing this. Instead, we need to start treating customer relationships like any other human relationship. That means we need to *slow down to speed up.*

THE CONTEXT OF CONNECTION

Slowing down to speed up is about how you follow up with people. If you're putting out great information that helps your buyer persona with their pain point, then your marketing team should be generating contacts in your database. Your sales team can then follow up, but they should approach those contacts with more value, honoring the context of the connection.

For example, they might say something like, "Mary, I see you attended our webinar on improving profitability in your organization. We think one of the tools talked about in the webinar would be a great asset for you. Let me know if you would like a copy. It's an analysis tool that many of our clients have used to gain clarity on ways to quickly increase profitability."

The engagement is about providing value based on where the person is at in their relationship with your brand—the behavior that Mary has demonstrated—and honoring that context. Contrast this with the way most sales teams operate today, completely ignoring the context and immediately pushing hard to get a long-term commitment. Nothing in Mary's behavior thus far says, "Contact me. I want a price quote right now." You have to respect that and follow up appropriately.

Remember, it's a mindset of service at every point of the customer journey. If someone is an existing customer, when you call them it shouldn't be to sell them something. Occasionally, you might want to upsell something you believe will meet a need, but your regular outreach with them should be primarily focused on making sure they're happy and making sure they are being treated well by everyone in your organization, followed by adding value somehow. For example, "I heard you mention a challenge you're dealing with during our last meeting, so here's a book that might help—or here's a person who might be a resource for you."

You don't want every interaction customers have with your company to feel like a sales pitch. Otherwise, they will quickly come to dread engaging with you. Find ways to add value and further the relationship.

Treat your prospects exactly the same way. Lead by having their interests in mind. Begin by looking for ways you can help and build a relationship from there.

As soon as you engage with DigitalMarketer, the leading providers of digital marketing training, they start following up by providing various forms of help. Even before you join their Certified Partner Program, they provide free content, invitations to conferences, and ways to interact with the community and ask questions.

You're already getting a lot of value from the company long before you spend a dime with them. When you finally decide to become a member, you already know you will get a ton of value for your money. "If they've done all of this for free," you think, "imagine what they'll do once I pay them!"

When you serve customers in this way, your progress might slow down initially on the micro-level, but your relationships on the macro-level will speed up. The prospects entering your pipeline will be real and ready. Even though you are putting fewer people into your pipeline, you are attracting more people who are ready to do business with you. After all, what's the point of having more in your opportunity pipeline if most of what's in there is worthless?

CHAPTER SIX

TOP-DOWN OPTIMIZATION

When most people think about developing a marketing and sales system, they think of it as a funnel, with the top of the funnel representing the early stages of the relationship with customers. As customers move closer to becoming committed buyers, they move deeper into the funnel. Strangely, this evokes the image of someone spiraling down a drain.

I prefer to think in terms of elevating relationships, where the ground level is strangers, and the pinnacle is raving fans. In the Digital Utopia Methodology, we've identified seven relationship levels. From lowest to highest, they are: stranger, visitor, lead, qualified, opportunity, customer, fan.

Rather than focusing on the lower levels, I encourage top-down optimization—put most of your focus into your fans. Let's face it, your fans buy more from you, they buy your best stuff, they talk about you online positively, and, in so doing, they help you grow your brand.

This perspective is flipped from the norm, and the buyer persona is key. Everything you do is built around that buyer persona, not just marketing and sales but your offering, your organization, and everything else. Your focus on the top is about figuring out what it takes to create raving fans. If customers aren't becoming raving fans, then you need to start optimizing there. When you start there, you will end up bearing a lot more fruit for less money than if you focus most of your effort on trying to turn strangers into visitors.

Suppose your brand gets 10,000 clicks on your digital ads, and out of those 10,000 clicks, you gain one customer. If you set a goal to gain ten customers by focusing on increasing the number of clicks, now you have to get 100,000 clicks. That's going to be very expensive.

However, if instead you simply optimize what it takes to create a customer, you might be able to get ten customers out of 10,000 clicks. Even if you only get half of your goal, you've still created far better ROI by optimizing from the top down.

Additionally, if you don't start at the top, then you're driving people into a system that will never convert at an optimal rate. No matter how much you invest in elevating visitors, having a bad offering in the mix will act as a constant hindrance to creating committed fans. Ultimately, you might as well just set your money on fire.

Working from the top down means fixing your product or service, doing whatever it takes to create raving fans by going above and beyond what is on the invoice. I'm not suggesting that you should stop marketing. I'm recommending that you focus first and foremost on optimization at the very top.

FIXING THE PRODUCT BEFORE FIXING LEAD GENERATION

I spoke to Ronn Cort, COO and President of SEKISUI Polymer Innovations, makers of KYDEX Thermoplastics. Surprisingly, his company doesn't have any salespeople in their organization, and their sales funnel is an hourglass. In a sales hourglass—as opposed to a funnel—the process doesn't end when the customer signs a contract. Instead, the company continues to engage customers to create a deeper relationship by continuously adding value long after the sale is completed.

The primary goal of SEKISUI is to show their target buyers that the cost of doing business is higher without them, and they provide an impressive list of reasons why this is true. Their actual product offering is at the end of that list.

They have embraced a process called Quick Response Manufacturing (QRM), which is a strategy that greatly reduces lead times in all phases of manufacturing, enabling them to provide customer-engineered products much faster. It's a model built entirely around the customer.

Their competitors require orders of at least 5,000 pounds, and they have lead times of six weeks to four months. SEKISUI has flipped this on its head, creating customized orders that can be as low as 600 pounds and shipped within twelve days.

They have entirely rebuilt their business around "digital natives," customers who are fully indoctrinated to use technology in every area of their lives. They recognize this as the new normal, so they raised capital to redesign every aspect of their company accordingly. Anyone can go to their website and figure out the cost of goods and materials. The company values *time* above anything else, and customers are thrilled to pay more to get their order sooner.

According to Ronn, "Ten years ago, I would have said

no one would pay more for shorter lead times, but today, it is baked into the DNA of buyers thanks to companies like Amazon."

Although they are a boutique manufacturer, large companies are seeing the value in what they do. Leaders of multi-billion-dollar companies have approached SEKISUI to learn how they've reinvented the way they do business, so they can emulate SEKISUI's growth model.

They have baked innovation into their culture. Whereas most organizations simply respond to customer requests and call it innovation, SEKISUI proactively innovates and then takes their ideas to their customer base. They put their money where their mouth is.

As a result of this approach, they are enjoying 40 to 50 percent market shares—even as high as 80 percent—in key markets. Their customers have changed their own business models as a result of the way SEKISUI does business, which has reduced overall costs for customers. Consequently, even though SEKISUI's products cost more than their competitors, customers are actually saving money as a result of the transformation.

Retention at the company is extremely high, with less than a 1.2 percent return rate. Their on-time delivery rate is an impressive 99.2 percent, and their employee turnover rate is 10 percent (compared to the average of 30 to 40 percent). Three years ago, the company made $149 million, last year they had grown to $186 million.

Bear in mind, SEKISUI's core product was invented in 1965, and it hasn't changed much. However, by focusing on the way they do business around the customer, they have radically changed everything. In a B2B manufacturing company, they have created an unparalleled experience for the customer, and it has made all the difference.

The most fundamental change they made was to pull all of their sales and customer-facing employees off commissions. Once employees stopped worrying about things like territory and splitting commissions, they could work together for the entire company. Instead of training people to be "hunters" or "harvesters," they start with their existing customers and leverage what they already have. This flies in the face of how everyone else does business.

As Ronn Cort says, "Client problems are almost never about the offering. Most of the time, they have to do with their systems and approach. If you can help your customers become better at their systems and approach, you will win. Let your products become a vehicle for bringing out those fundamental changes."

CHAPTER SEVEN

COMMITMENT AND CONSISTENCY

Suppose you want to get in shape, so you sign up for a gym membership. During the first month, you go to the gym consistently. It's not easy. You're sore, you're tired, and you're frustrated. As a result, by the second month, you're going less frequently, skipping a day here and there. During the third month, you only go to the gym three times in total.

What if, by the end of the third month, you were to say, "Working out at the gym is a waste of time. I'm not seeing any real results in the mirror." Wouldn't it be irrational to blame the gym for your poor results? You simply didn't put in the consistent hard work necessary to achieve the results you wanted.

It's the same in almost every area of life. If you don't do the work consistently, you don't get the results. Despite this basic truth, I am amazed at the response business executives all over the world have to their marketing efforts. They adopt some tactic, give it ninety days, and look at the results to decide if they should continue. Nothing amazing happens in marketing in ninety days, so setting these short timetables is entirely arbitrary.

In fact, if you look at the beginnings of the organizations themselves, you'll probably find that their first ninety days were pretty lackluster. It takes years for most organizations to begin making real progress. Why, then, do companies adopt such short-term expectations when it comes to marketing? Logic and reason seem to go right out the window, and suddenly leaders start thinking, "There must be some marketing agency out there that can come up with the right campaign, or the right verbiage, or the right tactic to produce immediate results—something we can just turn on and it'll work."

Marketing doesn't work that way. *Nothing* works that way.

THE ROI OF MARKETING

It's so important to get a healthy view about the ROI of marketing. Consider the following graph. On the X axis, we have length of *time*. On the Y axis, we have the *effort*, which means the hours, money, and resources you invest.

If you put in high effort consistently for years, you will start to experience ROI on your efforts. However, before you get to that point, there's that triangle area on the chart where you experience negative ROI—let's call it the "Triangle of Pain." That's the place that most companies never get past. Company leaders put in a few months of effort, look at the results, and say, "Well, this is a waste of time and money, so forget it. We'll start over with something else."

That, however, is the nature of a hamster wheel: constantly starting over and never getting past the break-even point. You have to take the time to build equity and let your brand start to work for you. Eventually, all of the audience-building you've done will become a trickle of positive ROI and then a gushing stream. If you keep starting over, you will never build momentum.

That Triangle of Pain is where your brand is born. All of the people above the ROI break-even point get the glory, but the truth is, the real glory belongs to the people working below the line. The people who pour their time, energy, and resources into the Triangle of Pain to make long-term momentum possible.

This is the paradigm shift that companies need to make when it comes to investing in marketing and sales. Everyone wants to avoid the Triangle of Pain, but you can't. There is no shortcut. Every time you try to take a shortcut, you're just spinning the hamster wheel again.

This is how the ROI of marketing works, but, in reality, it's the ROI of *everything*. This graph could apply to just about any effort. Think about it. What's the ROI of getting in shape? As I said, three months of increasingly sporadic gym attendance won't do it. You need to start getting up at five in the morning to work out, but, more importantly, you have to stick with your exercise routine for a long time before you start to see major changes.

Consistently working out—day after day, month after month, year after year—will eventually produce amazing results. Everything you've done, all the hard work, will begin to pay off, and the day will come when you look in the mirror and see a dramatic difference.

The amount of effort you put in after the break-even point doesn't change. You're putting in the same amount of work, but suddenly you're starting to see the results you'd hoped for. This is what companies get to enjoy when they stick it out. At this point, some leaders will start saying things like, "What are the marketing and sales departments doing? All of a sudden, we're driving so much ROI. Has something changed?"

In reality, nothing has changed. They've just been consistent long enough that it's starting to pay off. Suddenly, the trickle becomes a steady flow. It's the point at which brand starts to work for you. People start talking about you, and they start responding to your calls-to-action. From this point on, if you continue with the same degree of consistent effort, that flow of return is going to increase.

So many executives never get to that point because they are desperately trying to avoid the Triangle of Pain. They never push past the break-even point, so they never enjoy the fruits of their labor. Tragically, when you dump a strategy, you start back over at zero. All of those executives trying to avoid the Triangle of Pain are just cycling back through it over and over.

There's simply no avoiding it, just like there's no avoiding the early days, weeks, even months of a new workout routine where you're tired and sore, struggling to stick with your diet, depriving yourself of delicious cheese-burgers, and moaning about getting up every morning but not seeing any difference in the mirror. Ironically, most businesspeople understand this about getting in shape, but somehow the logic doesn't transfer to the world of business.

You can't escape the Triangle of Pain. If you want to get past it, you have to be willing to *push through it*.

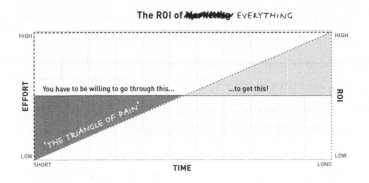

The ROI of ~~Marketing~~ EVERYTHING

ACCELERATING GROWTH

At this point, you could simply take the principles I've shared in this section and apply them to what you're already doing. Drill them into your organization until you begin to change the overall mindset. If you do, you will experience better results, even if you don't choose to implement the framework presented in Part Three.

However, in the next part of the book, I will share a blueprint you can build upon, with actionable steps you can take to begin making progress toward your growth objectives to help get your team on the same page once and for all. The end result will be a holistic strategy that creates a digital utopia of ongoing, consistent growth and ROI.

PART THREE

IMPLEMENTATION

CHAPTER EIGHT

THE DIGITAL UTOPIA BLUEPRINT

In the twenty-plus years I've been in sales and marketing, I've seen the development of some amazing technologies that are empowering people like never before. Solopreneurs and companies with small budgets have access to an increasing number of channels, allowing them to compete with even the biggest players. The landscape has changed dramatically.

However, we've reached a point where the abundance of tools and the number of available channels has become overwhelming. Everyone seems to be confused, and companies are so obsessed with finding the right tactics amidst all the options that they've forgotten what is most important.

What's most important is creating a strategy to better serve your buyer by letting them drive everything you do.

To help you do that, I want to introduce you to a tool you can use to build that strategy. It's called the Digital Utopia Blueprint, and it will guide you through the process of developing **one** digital brand experience for **one** buyer persona around **one** pain point or topic. I will walk you through each of the levels of the blueprint, so you can elevate the relationship with your target buyer persona and create raving fans in the process.

KEY TERMS OF THE DIGITAL UTOPIA BLUEPRINT

To download a free copy of the Digital Utopia Blueprint, which you can use to apply the strategy discussed in this book, go to BuildingYourDigitalUtopia.com.

Buyer Persona: The one person you're going to engage through content and offers. This is your ideal customer.

Business Math: The fundamental economics of what it's going to take to drive engagement and, ultimately, create customers at a profitable rate.

Digital Brand Experience: All of the content, offers, and campaigns architected around one buyer persona and one pain point (as mapped out on your Digital Utopia Blueprint).

The Digital Utopia Methodology

Buyer Persona and "Business Math"

BUYER PERSONA

Name: President Pete

Description: President of a $5M B2B technology firm

Age: 42

Gender: Male

Income: $175,000

Location: Phoenix, AZ

Education: B.S. from ASU

Watering Holes
- Social: LinkedIn, Facebook
- Print: Wired, Inc, Forbes
- Online: Mashable, TechCrunch
- Events: Creative Techs, IoT Summit
- Memberships: EO, Tech Execs Forum

Influencers
- Gary Vaynerchuk
- Cameron Herold
- Verne Harnish

Goals
- Increase revenue
- Increase profitability
- Drive marketplace awareness and positioning

Challenges
- Never enough time, people, budget—initiatives are always back-burnered
- Increasing competition creates lots of "noise" in the marketplace
- Technology moves faster and faster = disruption = CHAOS

Top 3 Questions
- How long does it take to see results?
- How much time is needed from me and my team?
- Who will I work with on your team?

Top 3 Objections
- I don't want a long-term contract
- Your pricing is more than I wanted to spend
- We have to get our new website launched first

Focus Pain Point

Pete has tried lots of things when it comes to marketing, but he is frustrated that he hasn't found the formula for consistent, high-performance marketing. He has serious growth goals and knows he has to crack the marketing code.

Statement of Value

The Digital Utopia approach to digital marketing enables President Pete to go from a frustrated executive that can never seem to get his sales goals off his mind and even questions his ability to scale the company, to a confident, rock star entrepreneur that delivers consistent marketing and sales performance.

MONTHLY OBJECTIVES

Level	Quantity	Conversion
Customers	10	25.0%
Opportunities	40	25.0%
Qualifieds	160	25.0%
Leads	640	5.0%
Visitors	12,800	

ROI

MAXIMUM COCA ANALYSIS

	LTR	of	$120,000
×	GM	50%	
=	LTV	of	$60,000
×	COCA %	of	5%
=	COCA $	of	$3,000

GROWTH INVESTMENT

To acquire 10 customers per month, the "all in" marketing budget should be in the neighborhood of, but not exceed, $30,000/mo. (COCA $ x Customers).

MAXIMUM PAID MEDIA CPCs

Based on a max COCA of $3,000, average Cost per Clicks (CPCs) should not exceed: $2.34

The Digital Utopia Methodology

Experience Worksheet

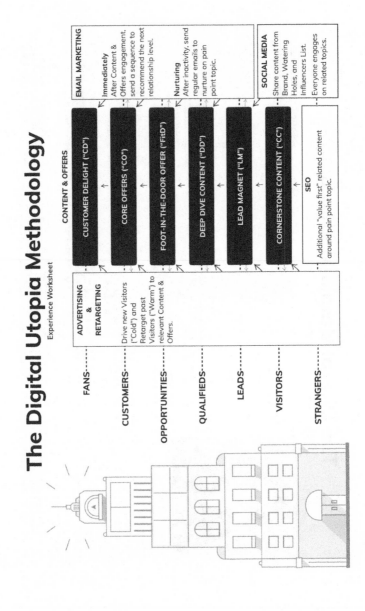

CONTENT & OFFERS

EMAIL MARKETING

Immediately
After Content & Offers engagement, send a sequence to recommend the next relationship level.

Nurturing
After inactivity, send regular emails to nurture on pain point topic.

SOCIAL MEDIA
Share content from Brand, Watering Holes, and Influencers List.

Everyone engages on related topics.

CUSTOMER DELIGHT ("CD")

CORE OFFERS ("CO")

FOOT-IN-THE-DOOR OFFER ("FitD")

DEEP DIVE CONTENT ("DD")

LEAD MAGNET ("LM")

CORNERSTONE CONTENT ("CC")

SEO
Additional "value first" related content around pain point topic.

ADVERTISING & RETARGETING

Drive new Visitors ("Cold") and Retarget post Visitors ("Warm") to relevant Content & Offers.

FANS

CUSTOMERS

OPPORTUNITIES

QUALIFIEDS

LEADS

VISITORS

STRANGERS

ELEVATING RELATIONSHIPS

Practically speaking, how can we create value in such a way that we elevate the relationship with our target buyer at every step? Traditional funnels are mostly focused on metrics, conversions, and optimization. While those things are important, they don't lead the strategy.

The problem with the old funnel is that people almost never flow through the steps of the funnel perfectly. An individual might flow down, then back up, then flow down again. It's rarely a direct linear path from end to end. This reality has led many in the industry to declare, "The funnel is dead!"

Relationship levels, on the other hand, will never be dead because they are based on the normal progression of human relationships. These relationships form the *core* of your digital growth blueprint.

Utopia is defined as an imagined community in which everything functions perfectly at every level. That is the ideal we strive toward at every relationship level with our contacts. We've been speaking of this philosophically, but now we're going to speak of it in terms of implementation. To begin, I recommend mapping these specific relationship levels in your database, so you know where all of your contacts stand.

Specifically, there are seven relationship levels in your digital ecosystem. Notice that they are listed in reverse order, with fans and customers at the top. That's because it's a relationship-driven focus, and the highest relationship you can have is a fan. The seven levels are:

- Fans
- Customers
- Opportunities
- Qualifieds
- Leads
- Visitors
- Strangers

As you can see, at each of these seven levels, your buyer has a heightened relationship with your brand.

While this may look like any other marketing-to-sales funnel (in reverse order), the five core philosophies we spoke of in Part Two (Service Mindset, Hyper-specificity, Slow Down to Speed Up, Top-Down Optimization, Commitment, and Consistency) are a major aspect of what makes the Digital Utopia Methodology so special. When you apply these philosophies, you create a tightly-focused *experience* that allows your target buyer persona to move from one relationship level to the next in a natural, logical manner, so much so that it becomes your buyer's idea.

Let's take a look at each relationship level, starting at the bottom, because it will be easier for you to understand them from the buyer persona's experience. Remember, these relationships are at the core of the Digital Utopia Methodology.

When reading through each of these levels, keep the idea of *hyper-specificity* in mind, because elevating relationships is about honing in on *one* buyer persona and the *one* pain point you are solving for that buyer.

ELEVATE STRANGERS INTO VISITORS

To elevate a stranger into a website visitor, the goal of your content should be to drive awareness and engagement around helping your buyer persona take steps toward alleviating their specific pain point. At this stage, you should produce content that shows differentiated value in the marketplace. To some extent, it's okay to produce content that is similar to your competitors' content, but at this level you're better off showcasing your brand's differentiated approach to the pain point.

We refer to content at this level as "Cornerstone Content."

Examples of Cornerstone Content include:

- Blog Posts
- Videos
- Infographics
- Case Studies
- White Papers
- Podcasts

When done right, cornerstone content goes beyond content that simply fills an "SEO gap." Instead, it exposes your brand's unique philosophies and approaches and communicates the message, "Here is how to solve your pain point." Bear in mind, making this content well requires having the lens of a *teacher*, not a promoter.

REAL WORLD EXAMPLE

Empyr, a technology company that enables companies to generate more revenue and delight their users with card-linked offers, has a buyer persona named Loyalty Liz. Liz is a VP of Loyalty Programs at a retail chain who wants to increase customer retention.

The challenge for Liz is that it's very difficult to clearly demonstrate ROI for loyalty programs. She knows she must come up with a solution, because her executive team expects measurable growth from her channel. Liz is in the early stages of discovering what her options are, and she's heard about "card-linked offers," but she has no understanding of the mechanics of how they work and no real sense of how costly they are to implement.

To help Liz, Empyr invested in the development of a robust piece of content that provides her with everything she could possibly want to know about card-linked offers: what they are, how they work, how to implement them, the investments required, examples of ROI, FAQs, and more. This piece of content was written from a place of pure education—it's not a sales pitch. Instead, it aims to arm Liz with the education she desires around card-linked offers. Empyr knows that this approach makes for the start of a great relationship.

ELEVATE VISITORS INTO LEADS

Once you have a visitor who engages with your cornerstone content, you can elevate them into a lead by providing additional value related to the content they are consuming. This additional value should be an asset or resource that helps your buyer persona take a deeper step toward solving their specific pain point.

We refer to content at this level as a "Lead Magnet." Lead Magnets should be much more valuable than your cornerstone content.

Examples include:

- Templates
- Tools
- Calculators
- Self-Assessments
- Checklists
- Audit Worksheets
- Blueprints/Cheat Sheets

The best lead magnets are those that provide a *missing link* to your Cornerstone Content. For example, your cornerstone content might be a blog post that teaches a concept for overcoming *pain point X*, so the lead magnet would be a tool that makes the process of solving the pain point easier. This lead magnet content continues to communicate, "Here's a resource to help you do it."

REAL WORLD EXAMPLE

My digital marketing agency, Digitopia, has a buyer persona named Marketing Mary. Mary is a marketing director who wants to get more out of her website and related digital marketing efforts. With limited resources, she needs to address the low-hanging fruit first and foremost.

To help Mary figure out what her low-hanging fruit is, Digitopia offers her a free website grading tool which instantly shows her how her website fares when it comes to technical, mobile, SEO, and security performance.

From there, Mary can start tackling immediate issues that are hindering her website's performance.

ELEVATE LEADS INTO QUALIFIEDS

At this level, you've engaged with them in such a way that they're now a contact in your database, whether through a social message exchange, a form on your website, or by email. You now have a way to communicate with them, but just because the buyer persona is a lead in your database, it doesn't mean your job is complete. You should continue providing focused value to elevate the relationship. To do this, offer them additional content, tools, and resources that give deeper education about how to solve their specific pain point.

We refer to content at this level as "Deep Dive Content."

Examples include:

- Videos
- Webinars
- Case Studies
- White Papers
- Books/E-books
- Online Courses
- Offline Events

Buyer personas who engage at this level have demonstrated that this particular pain point is very important to them, and they've taken these steps on their own without a high-pressure sales pitch. A lead at this level can become "qualified" when, combined with their behavior up to this point, they meet demographic and other contact characteristics that you define based on your business requirements.

The best Deep Dive Content focuses on providing compelling social proof that communicates, "See how someone just like you conquered or achieved X." The internal response of your target buyer persona should be, "Yes, this is what I want, and they're just like me, so I can achieve this, too. I have to know more!"

REAL WORLD EXAMPLE

APM, an Australian workplace worker wellness and rehabilitation company, has a buyer persona named Manager Marisa. Marisa is an injury management manager at a large Australian corporation who wants to help rehabilitate employees so they can get back to work as fast as possible. She would love to be working on programs aimed at proactive employee wellness instead of spending most of her time on rehabilitation, but Marisa is stretched too thin. She knows that if she can be proactive with the employee base, rehabilitation needs will drop, creating a healthier workforce.

To help Marisa, APM continues to nurture her with a series of thirty-second explainer videos. These videos quickly educate Marisa on nuances to consider when crafting her rehabilitation assessments so workers end up with a more holistic rehabilitation plan that gets them back to work faster.

ELEVATE QUALIFIEDS INTO OPPORTUNITIES

Now that your buyer persona is a qualified lead, you can elevate them to an opportunity by offering to help them take a small but important step toward solving their specific pain point. This offer should be a natural next step that provides high value and little to no risk for your buyer persona.

We refer to an offer at this level as a "Foot-in-the-Door Offer."

Examples include:

- Consultations/Audits
- One-on-One Demonstrations
- Trials
- In-person Seminars/Events
- Estimates
- Samples
- Physical Books

As I keep saying, this isn't the time to make a sales pitch for your offering. Instead, connect this offer to their last action: "Now that you've done that, you should do this."

Here's what this looks like in practice.

> Hi Vickie,
>
> Now that you've learned how and why the Digital Utopia Methodology works, you should consider talking with one of our digital consultants about how to implement it within ACME Corp.
>
> I want to offer you a no-cost, no-obligation consulting session with one of our top consultants, who will help you figure out what it would take to implement the Digital Utopia Methodology in your company.
>
> At the end of the session, you'll have a clear understanding of the time, people, resources, and investment required—whether you work with us or implement it yourself—to take your digital program to the next level.
>
> Let me know if you'd like me to reserve a session for you!
>
> Thank you,
>
> Frank

The key with the Foot-in-the-Door Offer is to make it specific to the pain point that your content has been addressing. Generic offers that say, "Contact us," or "Let's talk," won't do. This offer must take the next logical step in your buyer persona's journey and experience with your brand. When done right, it will seem like a natural next step after they've seen the social proof that you presented with your Deep Dive Content.

In some businesses, this is a free offer, while in other businesses, the offer might require a relatively small monetary transaction. Either way, it shouldn't be one of your brand's core offers. Instead, it should be an offer to take real action now that they are educated about their pain point and ready to do something to fix it.

Remember, as the name implies, what you're trying to do at this point is demonstrate enough value to get your foot in the door. Your communication of this offer essentially asks, "Would you like to experience this kind of transformation, too? If so, take this important first step."

Buyer personas who engage at this level are very serious and deserve your highest level of attention, even if they ultimately can't or won't do business with your brand.

Simplexity Services, which provides accounting and back office services for start-up companies, has a buyer persona named Founder Finn. Finn is the founder of a start-up that has a big goal to become the next unicorn (a start-up with a valuation over $1 billion). Finn has gotten his company off the ground, but he needs funding to take it to the next level. There aren't unlimited opportunities to raise money, so Finn wants to make sure he goes in with his best foot forward. He's nervous—he can't afford to screw it up.

To help Finn, Simplexity offers a no-cost, no-obligation investor preparation consultation. During this consultation, a start-up expert will look at Finn's books and help him craft a plan to make sure his books are ready for a thorough investor review, so he can get the funding he's after.

ELEVATE OPPORTUNITIES INTO CUSTOMERS

Once someone has received so much upfront value, becoming a customer is the next natural, logical step for your buyer persona. It's the final step towards solving their pain point once and for all. Make an offer that demonstrates you are the ideal resource for that solution.

We refer to offers at this level as "Core Offers," and they are the core of what you sell in the marketplace.

As you engage your buyer persona at this level, here are some tips to ensure you successfully elevate as many people as possible to the next level.

- **Continue to provide value.** It's no longer ABC (always be closing). It's now ABV (always bring value). As your buyer persona has engaged with your marketing, they've experienced a ton of value. Continue providing value by being eager to help rather than pitch.
- **Crystalize your value proposition.** All of the hard work has been done. Your buyer persona is ready to buy from you. Don't screw it up by dumping a ton of information on them. Instead, focus on articulating concepts that can be easily understood and on what I call the "big-ticket items," which are the factors your buyer persona cares about most.
- **Make buying a little-to-no-risk proposition.** If you can eliminate all of the reasons your buyer persona would hesitate to do business with your organization, your chances of earning their business go through the roof. Social proof, guarantees, and friendly terms are just a few of the major buying decision factors to examine. When you don't win business that you otherwise thought you would, it's usually due to some level of risk you failed to mitigate. Your goal is to make the decision to buy an extremely easy one.

As I mentioned earlier, when you follow the Digital Utopia Methodology, the decision to become a customer will seem completely natural. You won't have to resort to old school sales tactics. In the end, you will win more of the right business and differentiate your brand along the way.

At this level, your offer is very natural and logical: "If you're really serious and want to step on the gas, let us help you achieve this transformation."

ELEVATE CUSTOMERS INTO FANS

Once you have earned a customer, don't stop offering value. While your company might have solved your customer's major pain point, there's always another level you can take them. This might be accomplished through additional core offers that help them go further, but they can also be free offerings that are available only to your customers—a "velvet rope," if you will.

We refer to offers at this level as "Customer Delight."

Examples include:

- Continuing Education/Online Courses
- Office Hours
- User Groups
- Private Online Communities

- Exclusive Content/Events
- Discounts/Perks with Partners
- Access to Exclusive Venues
- Industry Data/Reports

When you build your company around providing customers with this kind of value, you'll create raving fans. Let's face it, in a world where there's no shortage of options for your customers, your only hope of keeping them around for the long haul is to commit to customer delight programs that go beyond the invoice.

When you continue to deliver value after your buyer persona becomes a customer, you're saying to them, "Let's not stop there. Let's take your transformation to an even better place!"

REAL WORLD EXAMPLE

Eldorado Stone, an industry leader of manufactured stone, has a buyer persona named Distributor Dan. Dan is the owner of a distribution company that sells Eldorado Stone's products. Like any distribution company, it is important for Dan to stay up to date on what's happening in the industry.

To help him do that, Eldorado Stone coordinates an exclusive annual event for distribution partners that they call

Stone Summit. A "mini conference" of sorts, this event features education, networking, and entertainment in locations like San Diego, California, and Park City, Utah. While this event is a significant investment for Eldorado Stone, the fans created by it are priceless.

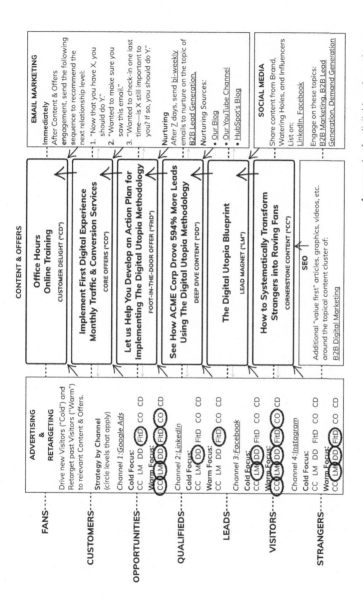

CONTENT & OFFERS

EMAIL MARKETING

Immediately
After Content & Offers engagement, send the following sequence to recommend the next relationship level:
1. "Now that you have X, you should do Y."
2. "Wanted to make sure you saw this email."
3. "Wanted to check-in one last time—is X still important to you? If so, you should do Y."

Nurturing
After 2 days, send bi-weekly emails to nurture on the topic of B2B Lead Generation.
Nurturing Sources:
- Our Blog
- Our YouTube Channel
- HubSpot's Blog

SOCIAL MEDIA
Share content from Brand, Watering Holes, and Influencers.
List on:
LinkedIn, Facebook
Engage on these topics:
B2B Marketing, B2B Lead Generation, Demand Generation

Office Hours
Online Training
CUSTOMER DELIGHT ("CD")

Implement First Digital Experience
Monthly Traffic & Conversion Services
CORE OFFERS ("CO")

Let us Help You Develop an Action Plan for
Implementing The Digital Utopia Methodology
FOOT-IN-THE-DOOR OFFER ("FHtD")

See How ACME Corp Drove 594% More Leads
Using The Digital Utopia Methodology
DEEP DIVE CONTENT ("DD")

The Digital Utopia Blueprint
LEAD MAGNET ("LM")

How to Systematically Transform
Strangers into Raving Fans
CORNERSTONE CONTENT ("CC")

SEO
Additional "value first" articles, graphics, videos, etc. around the topical content cluster of:
B2B Digital Marketing

FANS

ADVERTISING & RETARGETING
Drive new Visitors ("Cold") and Retarget past Visitors ("Warm") to relevant Content & Offers.

Strategy by Channel
(circle levels that apply)

CUSTOMERS

Channel 1: *Google Ads*
Cold Focus:
CC LM DD FHtD CO CD
Warm Focus:
CC LM DD FHtD CO CD

OPPORTUNITIES

Channel 2: *LinkedIn*
Cold Focus:
CC LM DD FHtD CO CD
Warm Focus:
CC LM DD FHtD CO CD

QUALIFIED

Channel 3: *Facebook*
Cold Focus:
CC LM DD FHtD CO CD
Warm Focus:
CC LM DD FHtD CO CD

LEADS

Channel 4: *Instagram*
Cold Focus:
CC LM DD FHtD CO CD
Warm Focus:
CC LM DD FHtD CO CD

VISITORS

STRANGERS

An example of a digital brand experience.

CHAPTER NINE

ENGAGING YOUR CORE

Once you have some or all of the core of your digital utopia in place, you're ready to engage your buyer persona. I say "some" because it's not necessary to wait until everything is perfect to start engaging your buyer persona. In fact, the demand for perfection is your enemy when it comes to engaging your target audience (or anything, really).

Because engagement tactics are constantly changing (and this book is about the strategy, not the tactics), we'll look at the various ways to engage your buyer persona in generalized "blocks" (the blocks that surround the core on the Digital Utopia Blueprint).

I will discuss each of these blocks philosophically, since

the tactics in each of these areas change often. No book on tactics would ever be worthwhile, because the information would be out of date the moment the book went to print.

Remember, this book is about the principles of elevating relationships and how to employ those principles to position and differentiate your brand, so let's simplify the conversation! In my opinion, the digital industry has made this process far too complicated. Simply stated, these strategic blocks can be grouped into two categories: engagement and reengagement.

ENGAGEMENT

Think of the following three blocks as the primary drivers of engagement:

- Advertising
- SEO
- Social Media

Let's take a look at each of them.

ADVERTISING

With a buyer persona thoroughly defined, use what you know about that person to get your content and offers in front of them on relevant websites that offer advertising opportunities.

Here are the major digital advertising paths you have at your disposal:

Search Engine Advertising

Search engines offer advertising that reaches people who are actively searching for specific information. That's the beauty of search engine advertising—your ad is placed in front of people who are actively searching for information related to your offering.

For these active searchers, it's a good idea to present them with your Foot-in-the-Door Offer first. While I fully believe in building a relationship before asking for the sale, active searchers are telling you that they're already warmed up. They're ready to go.

If someone is asking to take a big step, give them the opportunity by putting a Foot-in-the-Door Offer in front of them. If they don't take you up on the offer, you can always retarget them with Cornerstone Content as a way to build awareness and positioning so your brand stays top of mind when they're ready to take an appropriate next step in the relationship.

Social Media Advertising

Every social media platform offers you the opportunity to place content and offers in front of audiences based on criteria you define. Unlike search engines, the advertising you do here is proactive in nature, so the audience that sees your ads hasn't explicitly asked for anything. Because of this, it's a good idea to warm this audience to your brand by introducing them to your Cornerstone Content or Lead Magnet, depending on your business math, which we'll talk about later.

Other Online Advertising Opportunities

You should consider other online advertising opportunities. There may be an industry website that contains little more than subpar articles and a message board, but if most of your industry gathers there, it could provide better opportunities than some of the standard platforms, so explore your options. It's also possible that you're simply not able to profitably reach your buyer persona using search engines and social media platforms.

In either of these scenarios, you should consider looking at other online advertising opportunities. Finding them is as simple as searching the Internet for websites that cater to your buyer persona. There may be associations, discussion forums, events, or other places that already engage your buyer persona. You might find that the people on these websites are already in the right frame of mind, making them more receptive to your content and offers.

Important ROI Note: In some cases, the advertising cost when extrapolated out to the point of customer acquisition may not produce a positive ROI for you. If your content and offers are truly valuable and have been written and tested by experienced advertising-focused writers, you will need to lead with the next level up in your core: the Lead Magnet. You can get a clear sense of whether or not your advertising will produce a positive ROI by doing some basic business math using your marketing and sales conversion rates. We'll dive deep into business math in the next chapter.

SEO (SEARCH ENGINE OPTIMIZATION)

Unlike search engine advertising, where you pay to get in front of searchers with ads, SEO is about getting your content to appear organically below paid listings.

Out of all of the tactics in the digital marketing industry, no other tactic has such a "used car salesman" stigma as SEO. Unfortunately, the industry is directly responsible for creating this stigma. For years, SEO shops were secretive about what they were doing. Some wanted to keep a tight lid on their "secret sauce," and others resorted to "black hat" tactics: activities that search engines see as attempts to trick their algorithm into ranking a website higher in the search engine results.

It never bodes well when an industry adopts a secretive approach. Clients of SEO shops often felt like investing in SEO was a necessary evil, but they rarely had any idea what their SEO team was actually doing. On top of that, SEO shops often failed to set proper expectations. SEO is a long-term game, so it takes time to see results. However, most clients of SEO shops didn't understand this, so they wound up buying SEO with high hopes, often prioritizing SEO in front of advertising, even though advertising provides more immediate results.

In the end, they were almost always disappointed by their results, assuming that either their SEO team was incompetent or their SEO team had hoodwinked them. Neither of those assumptions are good for any industry.

Today, most SEO shops are on the up-and-up and very open about what they do. Unfortunately, the damage has already been done, so SEO remains one of the more suspicious digital marketing tactics for potential buyers.

Despite this, SEO continues to be an important part of building your digital utopia. Just make sure you understand that it is a long-term game, so you'll need to measure ROI accordingly.

Since this book is not a technical manifesto for market-ers, when I describe the things you should be doing in regards to SEO, I'm not approaching it as a precise "how to." Rather, I'm going to provide an easy-to-understand overview that I call "The Five P's of SEO."

Step 1: Perform Keyword Research

Find out which keywords your buyer persona uses and determine which ones you have an opportunity to rank in.

Step 2: Produce High-Quality Content

Develop content that aims to be the most helpful resource on the Internet for a given topic—develop for humans, not search engines.

Step 3: Publish Your Content

Publish the content to your website, making sure it's for-matted for maximum readability.

Step 4: Promote Your Content

Gain immediate traction with your content by announc-ing it to your email database, social media followers, and so on.

Step 5: Procure High-Quality Links

Connect with webmasters of relevant, high-quality websites and ask them to link to your content as a valuable resource for their audiences.

As I said, there are many technical aspects of SEO that I have purposely left out, but my goal is to simplify SEO for non-technical people, providing an understanding of the process at a high level.

SOCIAL MEDIA

Unlike social media advertising, where you pay to proactively place your content and offers in front of target buyer personas, social media is about engaging people who have specifically elected to follow your brand's social media page or profile.

The problem with social media is that social media platforms throttle your content. In other words, when you publish content on your page, very few of your followers will see it, because social media platforms want you to pay them to promote your content. Yes, you have to pay them to promote your own content to your own followers. Even though the platforms are ostensibly free, promotion comes at a price, so keep that in mind.

Does that make it a waste of time to engage in unpaid social media activity? No, because some social media platforms have features you can use to build an online community, and your posts aren't throttled in these communities (as of this writing). The key is to develop a community around a specific topic that is of interest to your buyer persona. To do that, you'll have to create a resource that delivers value.

For example, I'm part of an online community for growth-driven entrepreneurs that provides a means of sharing information and resources about growing companies. Of course, the company that created this community hopes to sell us their services, but they almost never make a pitch in the group. The resource is so valuable that we are aware of the brand anyway, and that awareness is a positive for the brand.

REENGAGEMENT

Generally, you can think of the following two blocks as the primary drivers of reengagement:

- Retargeting
- Email Marketing

Let's take a look at each of them.

RETARGETING

Once your buyer persona has engaged with any of your content or offers, you can stay in front of them as they move around the digital universe. To do that, you retarget them with ads. This works the same as the "Advertising" section above, except you're offering next-level content and offers based on how they've already engaged with you.

Note: On the Digital Utopia Blueprint, "Retargeting" is grouped with "Advertising" as these two almost always go hand-in-hand.

This approach ensures that you remain relevant at every stage of the relationship. It's also an effective and affordable way to build overall brand awareness and positioning, particularly due to the fact that a large percentage of your buyer persona will not move to the next relationship level in a rapid fashion.

When this happens, you want to add proof and positioning content to your retargeting mix. This approach will help cement your brand awareness and positioning so that when your buyer persona is ready to take things to the next level, your brand will be top-of-mind.

EMAIL MARKETING

Email is a way to engage people who have already had some sort of interaction with your brand, whether that's something as minor as subscribing to your mailing list or something major like making a purchase. According to the Association of National Advertisers, email remains an effective tool in today's data-driven world:

> For years, there's been the expectation that email marketing would eventually go the way of the DVD, AOL, and other tech from the 1990s, especially as millennials and Gen Z gravitate toward social, mobile, and other communication platforms. But more than twenty years after the first branded email message hit inboxes, email marketing remains stout as a business-to-business outreach and lead-generation tool.[12]

This isn't limited to B2B. When executed well and delivered with relevance to engaged audiences, email consistently delivers the highest ROI. According to a 2018 survey by Litmus, "By most measures, the ROI for email marketing is roughly twice that of other digital channels—if not better—and blows away the returns

---

12 David Ward, "5 Trends in B2B Email Marketing," *Association of National Advertisers*, January 30, 2019, https://www.ana.net/magazines/show/id/btob-2019-01-5-trends-in-b2b-email-marketing.

seen with traditional media channels like TV, radio, and direct mail."[13]

It's important to send timely, relevant content and offers based on the behavior of the person you're engaging with. The Digital Utopia Methodology is about applying human psychology to digital engagement, so don't always be in your subscriber's inbox with a sales pitch. Be there to provide value based on what you know about them and their interactions with your brand.

There are five types of emails you should send to your subscribers:

1. **Immediate Follow-ups.** Whenever someone interacts with your brand, they should receive an immediate, specific follow-up based on their interaction. For example, if someone requests access to a free resource, your immediate follow-up should include an email that provides the resource they've requested, with one to three emails afterward to recommend the next logical step in the relationship. As I discussed earlier, don't forget the, "Now that you've done *that*, you should do *this*," framework.

2. **Welcome.** The first time someone enters your data-

---

[13] Chad S. White, "The ROI for Email Marketing: The Good News and the Bad News," *Litmus*, August 16, 2018, https://litmus.com/blog/the-roi-for-email-marketing-the-good-news-and-the-bad-news.

base, welcome them to the family. A quality welcome is a series of one to three emails that introduces your new contact to a human at your company, tells a story about why your company is passionate about what they do, and provides immediate value. This is your opportunity to let your subscriber know that your intent is to give value to them, not make constant sales pitches.

3. **Nurturing.** Most contacts won't take the next logical step in the relationship. It's normal for people to "hang out" at a relationship level for a while. When that happens, don't give up. Stay in front of them with valuable content and resources related to their topic of interest. As long as you're providing relevant value on a consistent basis, your brand will receive a build-up of goodwill that will help you stay top-of-mind when people are ready to engage. When crafting nurturing emails, remember that your content should reinforce the need for change. The number one "competitor" you have is status quo, so you'll have to help your buyer persona make the transformation from "do nothing" to "do something." Where possible, leverage third-party, non-competitive content to help you reinforce your key messages.

4. **Extraction.** If a contact has been disengaged for a long period of time, you'll want to make a last-ditch effort to extract some sort of value from the relationship. You've given a ton of value and, up to this point,

it has been a one-sided relationship. Now, it's time to get something back by asking for feedback, referrals, completion of a survey, or something similar. You can also use this as an opportunity to direct them to content and offers from affiliated partners, if you have those kinds of relationships in place. Contacts that are still unresponsive for a period of time after these last-ditch emails should be considered "dead" and marked for removal at some point based on your company's database maintenance preferences.

5. **One-offs.** Up to this point, we've talked about emails that are automated, meaning they are created and sent automatically based on certain triggers. One-off emails are emails you manually send on a periodic basis to deliver timely content, resources, and offers. These emails can be more like newsletters, containing a round-up of content, or more of an email "blast," focusing on one piece of information such as the announcement of a new offering, event, or resource. Make sure to segment your database to ensure these emails are relevant to your subscribers, of course.

Important note: Generally speaking, emails should come from a person, not a brand. You want your subscribers to know that there is a real human being on the other end. One-off newsletters or blast emails can come from the brand, but you still want them to seem like they were written by the person your subscribers are used to receiving emails from.

CHAPTER TEN

GETTING STARTED

So, what's the high-level process of getting started? In simplest terms, the process looks like this: assess, plan, build, drive, optimize, and grow. You begin with an assessment, which involves something I like to call "basic business math," and then you conduct a bottleneck analysis. Let's take a look at these two.

ASSESS YOURSELF

When assessing your company, you want to get a sense of your current situation. What is happening with your current marketing, sales, and service teams? Are they aligned, working together as one team? Are they on the same page, and do they get what they need from one another? How effective are the people and programs within these teams? If they aren't in alignment, you need to bring them in alignment before you do anything else. That's your place to start.

Whatever platform these teams are using, make sure the data is aligned. Do you have a way to align all of that data, both in terms of people and in terms of technology? You don't have to overhaul everything tomorrow, but you at least need to understand the current state of affairs with your platform.

Ultimately, you are aligning marketing, sales, and service to create maximum flow in your digital utopia system. That is how you create maximum flow in your digital ecosystem. Assess where you currently stand, so you know what remains to be done. What's working, what's not working, and where are the execution gaps?

BASIC BUSINESS MATH

Once you have an understanding of the current state of your marketing, sales, and service teams, it's time to do basic business math. The purpose of this step is to answer the following questions: What does it cost to acquire a customer in your business, and what is an acceptable cost?

Sadly, most businesses can't answer these questions, which means the funding they set aside for marketing and sales isn't based on a real acquisition number. However, this information is critical to ensure you engage in activities that will eventually provide positive ROI. You can follow along in your Digital Utopia Blueprint as I walk you through the process.

KEY TERMS

Cost of Customer Acquisition (COCA): The total average cost of creating one new customer.

Gross Margin (GM): The average percentage of money you make per customer after subtracting the cost of producing a good or service.

Lifetime Value (LTV): The total revenue (Lifetime Revenue) you can reasonably expect to make from a customer multiplied by the average Gross Margin Percentage.

Though you shouldn't expect overnight results from your first digital brand experience, you still want to start with eventual profitability in mind. If you don't have a target number, you will be flying in the dark. That target number is called *cost of customer acquisition* (COCA), and it refers to the total cost of your marketing and sales efforts to gain a customer. If you know that number, you can derive budgets for your digital brand experience and related campaigns with a reasonable expectation of profitability.

How do you determine your COCA? First, for a given digital brand experience, determine what your buyer persona is worth in terms of lifetime revenue. I don't recommend using *total* lifetime revenue, because the payback will take too long, even if the numbers make sense on paper. Instead, use a two- or three-year revenue number.

Once you have that number, multiply it by your *gross margin percentage* for that customer. This is the average percentage of money you make per customer after subtracting the cost of producing a good or service. Your customers might have a wide range of spending, so use a "garden variety" customer. That way you get a number that is middle of the road. Take your *gross margin percentage* and multiply it by your lifetime/two- to three-year revenue number. That will give you your *lifetime value* (LTV), the total profit you can reasonably expect to make from a customer. Once you have that number, determine what percentage of that lifetime value you're willing to carve out for acquisition.

Some companies settle on 5 percent, others prefer 10 percent, and some go as high as 20 percent or more. I would say 5 percent is the absolute low end, but 10 percent is best, if you can afford it. Twenty percent may work for companies that are aggressively going after market share, but the 5 to 10 percent range is ideal for most.

Once you've decided on the percentage of gross margin

that you're willing to carve out, multiply that percentage by the lifetime value number. That's how you arrive at your COCA number, which gives you the threshold you're willing to spend to acquire a customer. Finally, multiply that number by the number of customers you want to acquire.

Suppose your goal is to acquire a hundred customers. Take your COCA number and multiply it by a hundred, and the result is your digital brand experience budget. Now you can make budget decisions that are designed for profitability.

YOUR BASIC BUSINESS MATH

(Lifetime Revenue) x (average Gross Margin) = **Lifetime Value**

(Lifetime Value) x (Acceptable Acquisition Percentage) = **Acceptable Cost of Customer Acquisition**

(Acceptable Cost of Customer Acquisition) x (Desired Number of New Customers) = **Digital Brand Experience Budget**

Of course, marketing and sales budgets should also include non-acquisition activities, such as building long-term authority online or creating general brand awareness. However, the smaller the company, the more you need to budget for activities that directly contribute to acquisition activities. With an actual number, you can make informed decisions about this.

HOW THIS LOOKS IN PRACTICE

Suppose the ACME Corporation has a goal to win 100 more customers (based on their buyer persona) per year, and they determine that each customer is worth $100,000 to them, with a gross profit margin of 40 percent. They would put $100,000 in the lifetime revenue box, 40 percent in the gross profit margin box, and the resulting LTV would be $40,000. If the company is willing to invest 10 percent of their LTV, then their maximum COCA will be $4,000 (10 percent of $40,000).

Very quickly, the company has been able to determine they can afford to spend $4,000 per customer, so if they want 100 new customers, then their budget for the year on this particular effort should be $400,000 (or $4,000 times one hundred customers). They also know that if they spend $400,000 to get one hundred customers, it will be profitable for them.

ACME'S BUSINESS MATH

(Lifetime Revenue: $100,000) x (average Gross Margin: 40%) = Lifetime Value: $40,000

(Lifetime Value: $40,000) x (Acceptable Acquisition Percentage: 10%) = Acceptable Cost of Customer Acquisition: $4,000

(Cost of Customer Acquisition: $4,000) x (desired number of new customers: 100) = ACME's digital brand experience budget: $400,000

Too often, companies like ACME just start spending. They know they want one hundred new customers, but they fail to do basic business math, so they don't know how much they should spend to acquire them. I strongly encourage you to sit down right now with your executive team and work out your basic business math, so you can make informed decisions when designing your digital brand experiences. That way you know up front that you're going to be profitable.

BOTTLENECK ANALYSIS

Now that you have some concrete spending numbers, you must be strategic in deploying them. You probably won't be able to tackle the entire spectrum of your marketing, sales, and service all at once, so you need to determine which areas need more attention than others.

Your *conversion rate* is the number of customers that you move through your relationship levels. In a perfect world, you would have 100 percent elevation at each level, but you're likely going to have a much lower rate. Let's say you are currently at 10 percent, but your objective is to be at 20 percent. Doubling your investment at every level in order to make up the difference would be very inefficient and expensive. After all, you don't know if you're doing better at some relationship levels than others. You might be doing a great job of turning visitors into leads, but a comparatively worse job of turning leads into opportunities.

A bottleneck analysis will show you the levels at which your flow is restricted. To conduct a bottleneck analysis, look at the number of customers you are elevating per month at each level and compare it to your overall objective. Let's put some real numbers on this. For the sake of ease, we'll limit ourselves to the four relationship levels that represent the biggest and most common milestones: visitor, lead, opportunity, customer.

Let's suppose your goal is to create 100 new customers per month, but when you look at the numbers, you've only elevated 50. Somehow, you need to double your results from 50 to 100. Upon analysis, you learn that you're getting 80,000 visits per month to your website. You might be tempted to think, "Well, we just need to double it to 160,000 visits per month, and that will double our number of new customers from 50 to 100."

However, you need to do a bottleneck analysis to figure out what's happening at each relationship level. Start from the top and work your way down. Let's say you look at your customer level and find you had 200 opportunities during the month to translate opportunities into customers through follow up, content, and offers, but you only elevated 50. That's a 25 percent elevation rate. While this rate can be better, it's not terrible.

Next you look at how many chances you had to elevate leads into opportunities through follow up, content, and offers. Maybe you find that you have 800 leads in your database, and 200 elevated into opportunities. That's a 25 percent elevation rate, which is quite good. You're doing a great job of following up and showing value to contacts that have elevated to the lead relationship level.

Now take a look at those 800 leads and compare them to your 80,000 website visits. That's an elevation rate of one percent, so your bottleneck analysis looks like this:

- Opportunity to Customer: 25 percent
- Lead to Opportunity: 25 percent
- Visitor to Lead: 1 percent

At this point, it should be obvious where you need to concentrate most of your increased investment in order to reach your goal of 100 customers per month. What can you improve for visitors to convince more of them to become leads?

You don't need more visitors. You're getting plenty of them. You just need to do a better job of elevating them into leads in your database. That's your bottleneck. Now, instead of trying to double your investment at every relationship level, you can focus your efforts and prioritize the things that will open up the bottleneck. What buyer persona can you serve through a high-quality Lead Magnet on your website that will elevate visitors into leads in your database?

Instead of taking this focused approach, what companies often do in this situation is deploy $200,000 haphazardly across all sorts of initiatives. They'll spend more on emails, Facebook, and Google ads, and they'll do more blogging. Most of the money being spent outside of the bottleneck is wasted, because it's not addressing the problem.

Of course, the more money you have to spend, the easier it is to address multiple areas and speed things up, but only if you fully address the bottleneck first. You shouldn't deploy into other areas until you're putting enough effort into fixing the bottleneck. Even if you have a healthy budget, you have to deploy the dollars wisely. We no longer live in a world where big corporations are content to throw money around regardless of the metrics, because everything now affects the entire continuum of marketing, sales, and service.

No matter the budget, everyone has to perform to a number. If you're the head of marketing and you want to help your company create better relationships in the marketplace, you have to deploy those dollars in the most effective way possible, and the bottleneck analysis gives you a way to uncover where to prioritize your time.

DIGITAL BRAND EXPERIENCE PLANNING

Armed with the results of your basic business math and bottleneck analysis, you're now ready for digital brand experience planning. You can now prioritize your buyer personas based on the investment you know you have. Even if you have the resources to tackle all of your buyer personas at the same time, I recommend starting with *one*, so you can get it right. Start with a very narrow focus about whom *exactly* you're attempting to engage in the marketplace.

Once you've done that, you can begin researching ways to uncover where your buyer persona is on an emotional level. What's important to them? What buzzwords do they use? What struggles are they dealing with? What is the one focused pain point you're going to solve for them through this process better than anyone else?

When you have your buyer persona defined, you can flip to the other side of your Digital Utopia Blueprint and begin designing your *digital brand experience*. Remember, your ecosystem is about the alignment of marketing, sales, and service across all of your digital brand experiences.

With this process we've just discussed, you're going to have multiple digital brand experiences, one for each buyer persona and pain point. By prioritizing a single buyer persona and pain point, you are simply finding the best place to start. Now, you can architect your first digital brand experience.

The easiest place to start is with the Lead Magnet. Come up with an amazing tool or resource around the pain point that the buyer persona can use, and you will make the rest of your digital brand experience architecture much easier to construct.

Your Lead Magnet has to be something that truly begins to address the pain point—not just an e-book. While e-books are great for Deep Dive Content in order to gauge behavior, your Lead Magnet has to be good enough that someone will be willing to request it from your website, through chat, or by some other form of direct communication. It must not only have high *perceived* value but high *actual* value.

The best Lead Magnets are tools and resources such as calculators, software, templates, and training—all fully functional things that can be implemented. Get this right, and everything else will be easier. It could make or break your entire digital brand experience.

For example, at our company, we have a buyer persona named President Pete, who is the president of a $10 million B2B technology firm. He has tried to step on the gas with his marketing efforts, but he's frustrated that he can't fund a full marketing department. On top of that, everything is so confusing that he doesn't know where to begin. His approach is focused on tactics and he's scattered.

Our Digital Utopia Methodology is meant to help President Pete get strategic by providing a blueprint that he can use to get started. The blueprint is the tool in our Lead Magnet box, and with our tool in place, the Cornerstone Content writes itself. Simply explain or teach what the Lead Magnet does, then offer the Lead Magnet as something that makes what you're teaching that much easier.

For the Deep Dive Content, take the pain point solution

one step further by providing your customer with deeper insights on the pain point you're helping them solve. An easy way to fulfill this is to provide a video on how to use the Lead Magnet or a video that showcases a person or company using the Lead Magnet to solve their problem. It's important that your Deep Dive Content shows compelling proof of the solution, product, or approach you're educating the buyer about. Create compelling proof and your Foot-in-the-Door Offer will become a slam dunk!

Next, develop your Foot-in-the-Door Offer. You probably already have some way to initially engage people with your brand, so this offer shouldn't be that difficult to create. Be consistent with your customer's context at this point—they have engaged with your brand around a specific pain point and, as such, your offer to help shouldn't simply be, "Hey, want a quote?" Provide an offer to help that feels like a natural, logical next step.

If you've done it right up to this point, becoming a customer should be the obvious next step, which means it's time to sell the offer that solves their pain point once and for all.

With this information, you're ready to build your digital brand experience. If you don't have the funds, staff, or time to tackle everything at once, use your bottleneck analysis to prioritize your efforts. Build the most important content and offers, and bring the core of your digital brand experience to life. Leverage your website management tools to deploy your content and offers.

There are more marketing and sales tools available to you than I can possibly list here, so do your research to find the ones that are right for you.

If selecting the right tech or tools for your organization, goals, and objectives is overwhelming, we offer a free consultation session to help you narrow down your options at BuildingYourDigitalUtopia.com.

DRIVE AND OPTIMIZE

Now that you've built the core of your digital brand experience, it's time to *drive* and *optimize*, which is the ongoing, cyclical phase in which you are constantly engaging and re-engaging to ensure maximum flow through your digital brand experience. You will want to refer back to your bottleneck analysis to prioritize activities.

For example, if your bottleneck analysis reveals that your biggest problem is turning visitors into leads, an appropriate activity would be *retargeting*, which refers to ads that remind visitors about all of your great offers and content. Once you start generating more leads, then you can add email nurturing to the mix.

Ultimately, prioritization should always align with your biggest bottleneck. Once you're fully addressing that specific relationship level, you can deploy any money left over to the next bottleneck down the list, and so on. That's how you define your *drive activities*.

Once you're executing your drive activities, make sure to optimize regularly. Remember, the clarifying question in the Digital Utopia Methodology is always, "How do we elevate the relationship?" It's another way of asking, "How do we improve our conversion rates?" If your conversion rate is low, you're not providing enough value.

If you're providing enough value, elevating the relationship will seem natural and logical to your customer. With optimization, look at where you're not elevating relationships at an acceptable level (based on your history, trends, and benchmarks), and consider the value you are offering to customers.

As we said earlier, optimization begins at the top: turning customers into fans. That's the job of your entire organization, beginning with your executive team. Of course, the last relationship level that your marketing team will be able to directly affect is turning leads into opportunities, so that's the top level for them. If they find that very few qualified contacts are taking advantage of a "Foot-in-the-Door Offer," then they need to figure out how they can give more value to make those decisions feel natural and logical.

Always remember that marketing shouldn't operate in a silo. Marketing, sales, and service should all be aligned, but since each team has specific responsibilities, there will be points at which you need to have a seamless hand-off of specific tasks.

Even multi-billion-dollar companies have to prioritize their efforts. You may be able to tackle multiple digital brand experiences or drive activities at once, but no one has an unlimited amount of funds or team members. Always look at how your entire digital ecosystem is flowing, so you can identify the digital brand experiences that need the most help. Deploy your attention, effort, teams, and money into your bottlenecks—drive and optimize those places first and foremost.

A HEALTHY DIGITAL ECOSYSTEM

The final step in this process is growth. Once your first digital brand experience is up and running, it will get to a point where it's mostly in maintenance mode. That's the beauty of the digital world. A digital brand experience in maintenance mode continues to produce results for you, even as you turn most of your attention elsewhere.

Now it's time to deploy another digital brand experience and start the process all over again. Eventually, you will have multiple digital brand experiences in play. As long as your marketing, sales, and service teams are working in harmony together through this process, these digital brand experiences will work together to create a *healthy digital ecosystem* or, as I like to say, your *digital utopia*.

This is your digital growth system, and it's the way successful companies maximize flow, generating momentum for long-term ROI that will continue to pay off.

CONCLUSION

Remember, taking action is better than taking no action. You've no doubt read plenty of business books that have presented a wide range of growth philosophies, but in the end, what matters most is that you begin to take action. Ultimately, my message comes down to this: *you must execute.*

You must get into a rhythm of taking action instead of worrying constantly that the thing you're executing isn't perfect. The rhythm of consistent execution creates far better results than waiting, debating, discussing, and hypothesizing about some perfect approach.

When you're stuck in the hamster wheel, that cycle of trying something, deciding it's not perfect, stopping, and trying something else, you will never make progress. Of all the philosophies we've discussed in this book, the most important is the *commitment and consistency* philosophy. Start taking action now and stick with it. Get into the rhythm and stay there.

If you need some help taking those first steps, download the Digital Utopia Blueprint (if you haven't already done so). While you're there, you can also read the free educational material we've provided. You'll find plenty of content, tools, and other resources to help you get moving. You can find all of these at BuildingYourDigitalUtopia.com.

If these free resources aren't enough, or if you'd like more help and a more personalized approach to building your strategy, you can hire a Digital Utopia consultant. To do so, contact us at BuildingYourDigitalUtopia.com.

We live in a crowded and noisy world. There are many companies vying for your customers' attention, but you can start creating better relationships today. You can create a better brand experience. You can create raving fans. You can separate yourself from all of the noise in your marketplace.

Whatever you do, take that important first step, even a small step, toward building your own digital utopia today.

ACKNOWLEDGMENTS

I wish to acknowledge the following people for their help, support, and encouragement over the years:

MY FAMILY: FOR THEIR SUPPORT

- My wife, Cheryl
- My children: Ashlyn, A, Kobe, and Killian
- My Mom and Dad
- My extended family: Aunts, Uncles, Cousins, In-Laws

MY FRIENDS AND ASSOCIATES: FOR THEIR HELP

- Our Employees, current and past
- Our Clients, current and past
- Business Partners: Joe Freeman, Julien Brandt, and Arianne Brandt

- Past Business Partners and Associates: Andy Gerbing, Sarah Szilagyi, and Bob Weil
- EO Forum, FFK9: Ayal Shafran, Jasmine Powell, Noemi Kis, Amish Shah, Mark Wilson, Isaac de la Fuente, Dave Gerns, and Josh Bigelow
- Mentor: Jerry Stein
- Other Agency Owners: Nii Ahene, Chuck Phillips, Kevin Barber, Les Kollegian, Bob Ruffolo, David Smith, and Tobi Alli-Usman
- Ryan Deiss, Marcus Murphy, and the entire team at DigitalMarketer
- The "Dans" at HubSpot: Dan Tyre and Dan Vivian

ABOUT THE AUTHOR

Digital business expert **FRANK COWELL** has spent the last twenty years developing a growth strategy that systematically transforms strangers into raving fans in the digital age. His core belief is that businesses must shift from a "closing the deal" mindset to one of elevating relationships. Frank is CEO of Digitopia, a digital brand strategy agency located in San Diego. He works with CEOs, CMOs, and VPs of Marketing who are looking to implement strategic, systematic, and simplified solutions for growth. A self-taught programmer with a deep understanding of technology, he is also an energetic speaker on accelerating growth, brand differentiation, and digital marketing.

Made in the USA
Coppell, TX
29 July 2021

59657340R00090